THE QUIRKY GUIDE TO BIRMINGHAM

THE QUIRKY GUIDE TO BIRMINGHAM
A MELANGE FOR VISITORS & LOCALS.
UNKNOWN. UNUSUAL. UNFORGETTABLE.

R. J. HUTCHESON

The Quirky Guide to Birmingham

www.quirkyguides.com

First published by Quirky Guides in 2020.

Copyright © Quirky Guides 2020

Main text set in Baskerville URW.

The moral right of R. J. Hutcheson to be identified as the Author of this Work has been asserted in accordance with the Copyright, Designs and Patents Act, 1988.

All images and illustrations copyright © R. J. Hutcheson. The cigarette cards shown on pages 26 and 38 are reproduced from originals owned by the Author.

A catalogue record for this book is available from the British Library

ISBN 978-1-5272-7083-1

All rights reserved. No part of this book may be reprinted or reproduced or utilised in any form or by any electronic, mechanical or other means, now known or hereafter invented, including photocopying and recording, or in any information storage or retrieval system, without the prior permission in writing from the publisher.

All trademarks, where mentioned, are acknowledged. All brand and product names used in this book are registered trademarks or trade names of their respective holders. No permission is given by the publisher in respect of the use of any such brand or product names and such use may constitute an infringement of the holder's rights.

The what3words logo and 3 word addresses are used with the kind permission of what3words Ltd.

Although the Author has taken all reasonable care in preparing this book, no warranty is made about the accuracy or completeness of its content and, to the maximum extent permitted, disclaims all liability from its use.

Any omissions or errors will be corrected in a future edition.

Nothing in this book was published in exchange for payment or benefits of any kind.

Printed and bound in the UK by Biddles Books Ltd.

Acknowledgements

My gushing speeches at the doubtless abundance of forthcoming literary awards will include thanks to the following:

Darren and Geraldine for their early trials of some locations and for the loan of their photographic paraphernalia.

Emanuela and Rezam also for their early trials of locations and Emanuela's considerable skills with a red pen.

And Alison. For everything. Ever.

In Memorium

People of Brum I never knew whose stories will stay with me always.

Jane 'Ginny' Bunford
Nicola Dixon
Janet Parker
Private George Ravenhill VC

Jelly Bean Bull
A replica of The Guardian decorated with
Jelly Belly beans.
Ground Floor of Selfridges, Bullring

Contents

Introduction 1
One More Thing 2
Finding Stuff 3
1. Lingo 14
2. Playlist 16
3. Skyline 18
4. Feeling a Bit Drained 20
5. A Tale of Two Plaques 22
6. A Life in the Year of the Chinchillas 23
7. Interchange 24
8. Grave 36 26
9. Will of the People 30
10. Nose 31
11. Defenestration 32
12. Brumyanmarvellous 33
13. JFK 34
14. Post 36
15. A Very Buried Man 38
16. Getting an 'OO' 43
17. Sentinel 44
18. Going Underground 46
19. Acme 48
20. A Sunflower Among the Roses 49
21. Graffiti 50
22. Diamond Geezers 54
23. Listed 56
24. Keeping it Real, Bab 58
25. New Plaques, Please 60
26. The Last House in Birmingham 62
27. We Was Robbed 64
28. Flag 67
29. Battle Royal 68
30. The Final Victim 72
31. Walked All Over 74
32. The Long and Short of it 78
33. What a Relief 80
34. You Can See My House From Here 82
35. Destroyer of Worlds 84
36. Random Nuggets 86
Index 92

'The Guardian'
Bull sculpture at the Bullring
///skill.still.kind

Introduction

It was a bit embarrassing the first time it happened. When someone asked me what to visit in Birmingham. I wasn't working in the tourist information office but still, they could have expected a better response than the rabbit in the headlights look I offered.

After leaving the corporate world I followed my automotive enthusiasm and started a classic car hire company. Everything was fine and dandy and the cars would mostly be going to various corners of Britain for weddings and the like. Then, I had that encounter with the customer who was staying in Brum and looking for inspiration of where to go in their retro wheels.

I'm a Brummie born and bred but I had absolutely no idea what to say. I blurted something along the lines of 'Sutton Park's quite nice'. I knew I would have to be better prepared for the next time it happened.

When the customer returned they regaled the wonders of Brum they'd been able to see in spite of my assistance. Things I'd never heard of or not seen for a very long time. My curiosity was piqued when they told me that the lampposts near the Cadbury factory were purple to match the company branding. I'd always had a penchant for the more unconventional facts or places. When I visited Barcelona I regrettably never stepped foot inside the Sagrada Família but did find time to seek out the back street shop that made oversized papier-mâché heads for carnival season. I looked up those purple lampposts and one thing literally led to another and I soon amassed a plethora of under the radar stuff about Birmingham. Things I didn't need to know, but I was glad I did.

I hoped to combine my new knowledge with the car hire business to establish a self-drive quirky tour of Birmingham. That idea fell by the wayside and this book was conceived instead to ensure that the rest of the world was not deprived of this melange of Brum's unknown, unusual and unforgettable.

One More Thing

Fred L Worth wrote a book of trivia in the USA and included a fact that dishevelled, mac attired Detective Columbo's first name was Philip. Fred had made this up and knew it was incorrect. He included the fib as a means of trapping anyone who decided to copy his work.

It almost worked. Years later Fred sued the makers of Trivial Pursuit for millions as the Columbo 'fact' had made its way onto their question cards. Fred lost his legal battle but nonetheless I thought it would be a great wheeze (yes, I did used to read The Beano) to include a deliberate error in this book.

It's not a spelling or grammatical error (although I can't promise there aren't some of those too). Don't worry about being sent in the wrong direction, to something that doesn't exist or telling your friends porkies. I haven't made anything up – it's much more subtle than that.

No prizes for guessing either, so don't bother telling me. I already know.

Columbo's first name has never been spoken in the shows but some eagle-eyed viewers noticed that in a couple of episodes you can see his ID card which declares him as 'Frank Columbo'.

Finding Stuff

Finding a museum is usually quite straightforward. It's probably got a postcode, a crowd outside (pre-Covid-19) and a big sign saying 'Museum'. So, with a smart phone, sat nav or even an old-school map you'll probably find it.

But this guide is all about the quirkier places which are more difficult to pinpoint. Graves and plaques in the pavement don't have postcodes.

That's why I've used what3words to help take you to the exact location.

What is what3words?

what3words is the simplest way to talk about location. It is a global addressing system which has divided the world into 3m x 3m squares. Each square has a unique 3 word address composed of three words from the dictionary. This is easier to remember and share than some other location reference systems.

What does a 3 word address look like?

You'll find 3 word addresses throughout this book. They look like this:

///gazed.across.like

Three forward slashes are always placed before a 3 word address to help with visual identification. The words are always in lower case. You'll see the 3 word address written in different colours but this has no significance to the address.

How do I use a 3 word address?

The easiest way to use a 3 word address is to download the free app from www.what3words.com.

You can simply type in the 3 word address and the location of the 3m x 3m square will be shown on a map. If you don't download the app, you can do the same by entering the 3 word address on the what3words website.

what3words does not provide navigation instructions directly but if you click 'navigate' in the app you will be prompted to use an existing navigation system on your device (e.g. Apple Maps) which can be utilised to arrive at the 3 word address destination.

What will I find at the 3 word address?

The location of the 3 word address may contain the actual item from the book or the item may be visible from the location (e.g. the photograph in the book may have been taken from the 3 word address). Either way, the item in question should be unmissable from the 3 word address location.

Be careful out there

The vast majority of locations in this book are in public spaces or where the public has free access. A few locations are on private land but can be seen from the public spaces such as the pavement.

Some attractions are inside shops or shopping arcades. 3 word addresses are not available for indoor spaces.

Some 3 word addresses may encroach onto private land (e.g. a 3m x 3m square might overlap the public pavement and someone's garden). Please do not enter private land without permission. The inclusion of a location in this book does not give you permission to enter private land or buildings.

Access and availability to items can change over time, particularly with Covid-19, so please follow the restrictions in place at the time of your intended visit.

The map on the facing page shows the ten constituency areas of Birmingham. The boxes shown right, in the same colours, show the page numbers of chapters that include something of interest from the constituency area concerned. A chapter may cover more than one area so page numbers appear more than once.

1 City Centre & Ladywood
See chapters on pages:
14, 16, 18, 20, 22, 23,
31, 33, 36, 38, 46, 48,
43, 50, 56, 58, 60, 64,
74, 78, 80, 86

2 Perry Barr
See chapters on pages:
26, 56

3 Erdington
See chapters on pages:
16, 24, 31, 44, 56,

4 Hodge Hill
See chapters on pages:
56, 86

5 Yardley
See chapters on pages:
36, 56

6 Hall Green
See chapters on pages:
36, 54, 62,

7 Edgbaston
See chapters on pages:
56, 60, 72, 84, 86

8 Sutton Coldfield
See chapters on pages:
49, 62, 68, 80, 86

9 Selly Oak
See chapters on pages:
86

10 Northfield
See chapters on pages:
56, 78, 82, 86

4 | The Quirky Guide to Birmingham

approx. 13 miles / 22 km

approx. 16 miles / 27 km

M5 | **M6** | **M42** | **M6 Toll** | **M6** | **M42**

1. City Centre & Ladywood
CITY CENTRE
2 Perry Barr
3 Erdington
4 Hodge Hill
5 Yardley
6 Hall Green
7 Edgbaston
8 Sutton Coldfield
9 Selly Oak
10 Northfield

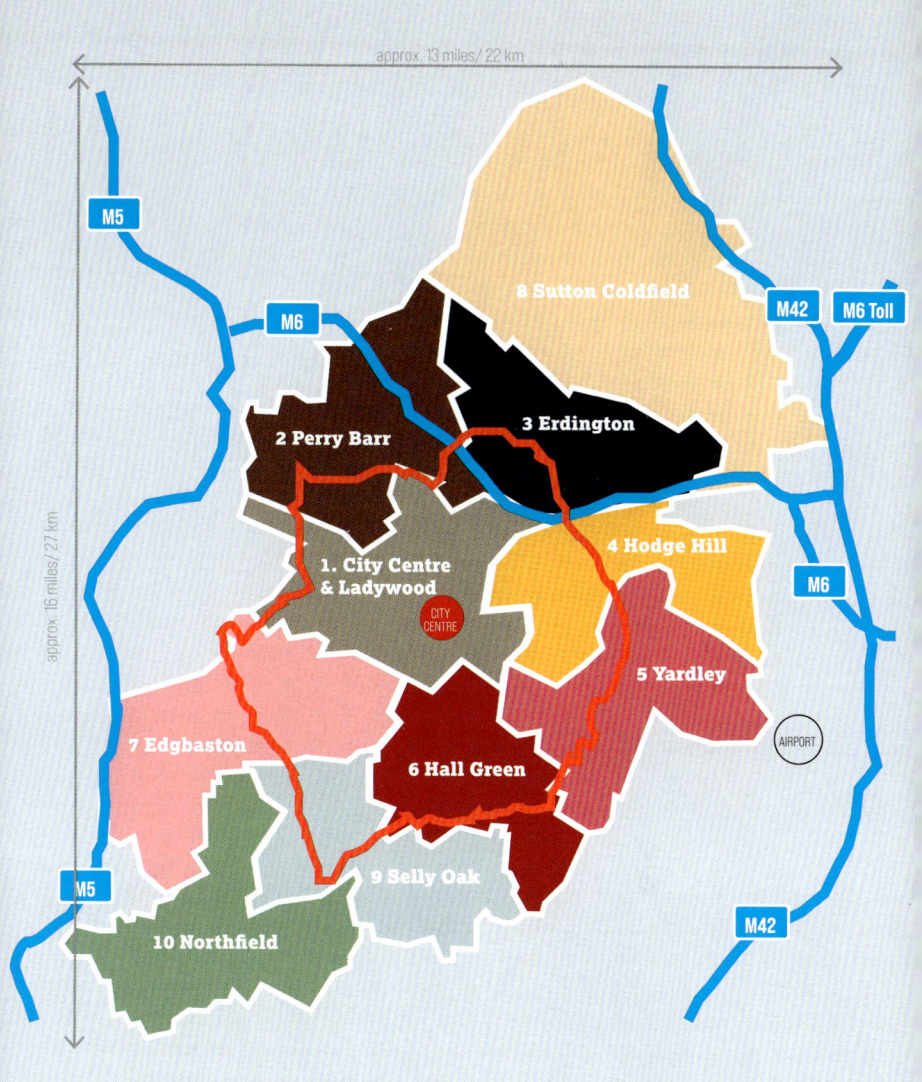

AIRPORT

━━━ The legendary No. 11 Outer Circle bus route. 27 miles with 266 bus stops.

The Quirky Guide to Birmingham | 5

The Library of Birmingham

'One has no great hope of Birmingham. I always say there is something direful in the sound.'

Mrs Elton
'Emma' by Jane Austen
1815

Inside Birmingham New Street Station/ Grand Central
City Centre

'Up yours Mrs Elton'

The Author
2020

Selfridges
///ranges.stay.body

'Birmingham has changed a lot...but for me it's still the centre of the universe'

Benjamin Zephaniah
2006

The Rotunda
///deputy.cowboy.candle

'That's more like it.'

The Author
2020

Chapter 1

Lingo

If you're a visitor to Birmingham it's helpful to understand a few useful words and phrases of the local language. Even if only to know not to hold violent thoughts the first time a stranger calls you Bab.

Proper Brummie	**Proper English**
A bit black over Bill's mother's	Dark skies look like impending rain
Ackchully	Actually. Often used as a redundant beginning of a spoken sentence. 'Ackchully, I'm going home'
A face as long as Livery Street	A very sad face
All (a)round the Wrekin	To take a long, convoluted route to arrive at a physical destination or the crux of an explanation
Bab	An oft used friendly term of endearment or greeting irrespective of age of the recipient: 'Alright Bab',
Babby	A baby or young child or, maybe, the youngest person present even if they're 50
Back of Rackhams	See explanation opposite
Bap	A round, soft bread roll (not a 'cob')
Buzz	A bus
Buzzinit	To use a bus as a means of travel to a destination e.g. Q:'How are you getting up town?' A: 'I'm buzzinit'
Carpet salesmen	See explanation opposite
Cob	A round, crusty bread roll (not a 'bap')
Floozie in the Jacuzzi	A part of 'The River' sculpture/ water feature in Victoria Square. See page 20
Gambol	Pronounced 'gam-bowl'. A forward roll, as in gymnastics
Island	A traffic roundabout
I'll go to the foot/ top of our stairs	An exclamation of surprise/ astonishment, good or bad
Mom	Mother. Never 'Mum'.
Never in the of pigs pudding	Something extremely unlikely to occur
Outdoor	A licensed shop where alcoholic beverages may be purchased for consumption off the premises. An off licence.
Piece	A sandwich. E.g. a piece of jam is a jam sandwich
Pigeon Park	See explanation opposite
Pop	A fizzy soft drink e.g. 'Mom is the pop man coming this Sunday?' (ask your parents).
Ramp, The	See explanation opposite
Tarar a bit	A parting salutation. Goodbye
Town/ up town	Brum city centre e.g. 'I'm goo-in up town on the buzz'
Up the wooden hill	Up the stairs (usually meaning to bed)
Yu wah	You what? Pardon, please could you repeat that?

Livery Street is approximately 0.5 miles long. It is, apparently, the longest street in the city centre (there are no 'roads' in the very centre). Longer streets are available – see page 62. Livery Street was used by Steven Spielberg for a car chase in the film 'Ready Player One'.
///organ.prices.struck

Rackhams is the old name of the city centre department store House of Fraser. It's only been 17 years since the change so many Brummies, like me, have been unable to adjust and still refer to the shop by the old moniker. 'Back of Rackhams' probably refers to an area that was once reputed to be a red-light district near the location of the store. This gave rise to many a schoolboy insult of friends' mothers working 'at the back of Rackhams'. Local brewer Two Towers produced an ale called 'Bhacker Ackhams' as homage to the phrase.///rooms.scary.also

AKA 'The Golden Boys'. This is the gilded bronze statue by local lad William Bloye. It depicts three of Birmingham's biggest hitters from history; Matthew Boulton, James Watt, and William Murdoch. The well-known landmark stood outside the old Registry Office on Broad Street for decades. They are not pondering a carpet but a partially rolled-up plan of a steam engine which they were famous for improving. The statue has been in storage since 2017 whilst improvement works are undertaken in the area.

Not the official name on maps but what locals call the place. This is the grounds/ graveyard of St Philip's Cathedral in the city centre where pigeons outnumber people.
///liner.smooth.factor

Another example of a name you won't find on maps but everyone knows what where it is. The inclined pedestrian access leads from New St to Grand Central. Well before social distancing was a thing, signs (and at one time, even loudspeakers) encourage people to keep to different sides when going up and down the ramp. Which everyone ignores. The official address of a business on The Ramp is Stephenson Place. But you won't hear anyone refer to McDonalds at Stephenson Place, just 'Maccies on The Ramp'. ///fantastic.lively.trap

The Quirky Guide to Birmingham | 15

Chapter 2

Playlist

Brum has a rich and varied musical heritage to rival any city in the UK. What better accompaniment to your tour than some of the music which has links to the city. Here's an eclectic mix tape from the past few decades.

Year	Title	Artist/ Group
1967	Nights In White Satin	Moody Blues
1967	Paper Sun	Traffic
1968	Flowers in the Rain	The Move
1973	I Wish it Could be Christmas Everyday	Wizzard
1974	How Does It Feel	Slade
1975	Funky Moped	Jasper Carrot
1977	Mr Blue Sky	ELO (Electric Light Orchestra)
1978	Handsworth Revolution	Steel Pulse
1980	Can't Get Used To Losing You	The Beat[1]
1980	Living After Midnight	Judas Priest
1980	Paranoid	Black Sabbath
1981	Good Morning Universe	Toyah Willcox
1982	Come On Eileen	Dexys Midnight Runners
1982	Pass The Dutchie	Musical Youth
1985	Kiss Me	Stephen 'Tin Tin' Duffy
1985	The Reflex	Duran Duran
1986	Pink Sunshine	We've Got a Fuzzbox and We're Gonna Use It !!
1988	She Drives Me Crazy	Fine Young Cannibals
1989	Kingston Town	UB40
1989	The Hoochie Coochie Man (from Kingstanding)	The Debonairs
1990	Suffer The Children	Napalm Death
1993	Boom Shack-A-Lack	Apache Indian
1996	The Riverboat Song	Ocean Colour Scene
1997	Bentley's Gonna Sort You Out	Bentley Rhythm Ace
1999	Outer Circle (see page 5)	Woodbine
2003	Superstar	Jamelia
2004	Fit But You Know It	The Streets
2014	Can We Dance	The Vamps
2017	Idle Stranger	Miccoli
2020	Quarantine Speech	Lady Leshurr[2]

[1] *Known as 'English Beat' in US and Canada and 'British Beat' in Australia*
[2] *Technically from Solihull. Which isn't Birmingham. See page 62*

This song features the 'Mellotron', an early music synthesiser (or more accurately, an electro-mechanical polyphonic tape replay keyboard) developed and manufactured in Birmingham in the 1960s. Numerous other artists have featured the instrument such as Oasis and The Rolling Stones but perhaps most famously The Beatles on the instantly recognisable opening of Strawberry Fields. The Mellotron continues to be used by artists due to its unique sound.

Those five Brum bands all played at the same music venue as did the likes of Led Zepellin, Pink Floyd, The Who, Elton John, T-Rex and Fleetwood Mac. America's Billboard magazine once proclaimed it number one rock venue in the world and John Peel was a regular DJ there. He commented that this was the best club in Britain for a while. This was Mothers Club, a modest first floor venue on Erdington High Street which was only open between 1968 and 1971.
///vines.locker.poet

This record should have been a real money maker for The Move. It was the first record (pedantry excluded) played on Radio One when the station started in 1967 but a risque promotional campaign completely backfired. Consequently, the band have never earnt a penny in royalties from the song. The band manager, Tony Secunda, arranged for a postcard to be distributed with artwork depicting the then Prime Minister Harold Wilson in an, err, compromising situation with his secretary. The PM sued, won and was awarded all royalties from the record in perpetuity. Wilson died in 1995 but the royalties arrangement continues to this day. Hundreds of thousands of pounds have been paid to charity on Wilson's behalf. As songwriter, Roy Wood probably lost out most.

Many believe that Heavy Metal music was a Birmingham invention and Black Sabbath were among the pioneers. Black Sabbath Bridge is located on Broad Street (photo above right ///maps.moons.memo).
Ozzy Osbourne's childhood home was 14, Lodge Road, Witton (photo above left ///purple.axed.member).

Chapter 3

Skyline

As Telly Savalas once said of Birmingham's skyline, with no hint of irony, 'This is the view that almost took my breath away'*.

One of the problems of getting a good panoramic view of a city is that you ideally need to be high up and often that means being in one of the buildings that you'd rather be in the photo itself.

The trick is to find a building high enough and in the right location but you don't mind if it's not in the photo.

Having scoured the city centre for a freely accessible structure which affords great views of the central Birmingham skyline, the final choice was the Markets Car Park. As it's a boring, concrete multi storey car park, it's fine that it stays out of your gaze and viewfinder.

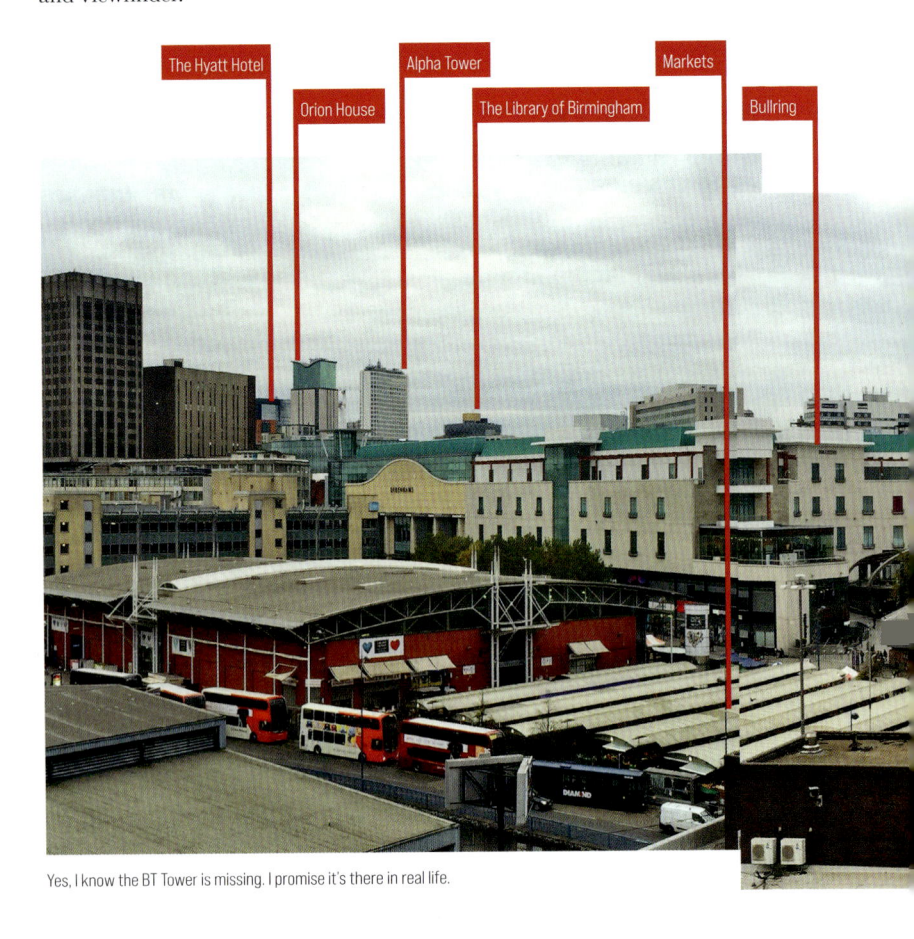

The Hyatt Hotel • Orion House • Alpha Tower • The Library of Birmingham • Markets • Bullring

Yes, I know the BT Tower is missing. I promise it's there in real life.

18 | The Quirky Guide to Birmingham

The photos below were taken from the very top floor of the car park – Level 14. The photos only show a partial view of the city but there is a very good 360 degree view for miles around the centre (weather permitting).
If you prefer a view of the city from further afield then see page 82.
At the time of writing the car park hasn't been demolished and pay & display charges apply for parking.

In the 1970s Telly Savalas was one of the most recognisable people on Earth thanks to his title role in 'Kojak' and for playing (spoiler alert) Bond's wife killing villain, Blofeld. In 1981 Savalas narrated a promotional film for Birmingham. Amongst other overenthusiastic phrases he uttered during the film was 'Riding the express elevator to the top of one of the city's highest buildings, this is the view that almost took my breath away'. Savalas had never stepped foot in Brum. To see the full film just type 'Telly Savalas Birmingham' into your favourite search engine and you'll find it.

Markets Car Park
Great views from the top floor
///spray.goods.analogy

The Rotunda

Selfridges

St Martin in the Bull Ring

The Quirky Guide to Birmingham | 19

Chapter 4

Feeling a Bit Drained

You might be wondering why, in a book about the quirky, more unusual sights of Birmingham you would be brought here, slap bang in the centre of Birmingham to one of the most visited and photographed places in the city. Well, even in Victoria Square you can find an oddity. In this case it is an unfortunate prediction which was set into stone around 30 years ago.

The centrepiece of Victoria Square (leaving aside the magnificent Council House, Town Hall and the statue of Queen Victoria) is a series of stone sculptures. One of these is locally known affectionately as the 'Floozie in the Jacuzzi'.

Unless you have known Birmingham for a while it may not be immediately obvious why this sculpture earnt its nickname or even its official name of 'The River'. A naked lady reclining in the square might explain the 'Floozie' part but there is a distinct lack of water and bubbles to conjure up images of a Jacuzzi. Floozie in the Jungle might be more apt now but originally this was constructed as a spectacular aquatic centrepiece.

An international competition was held to design a central water feature for the square, which was won by Dhruva Mistry. Construction was completed in 1994, when the square was officially reopened by Diana, Princess of Wales.

20 | The Quirky Guide to Birmingham

Thousands of litres of water should be leaving the Floozie's pool every minute and cascading down a terraced slope to a lower pool where there is a statue of a boy and girl facing each other and a fountain between them. Six large salmon depicted on the floor of the lower pool are now invisible. The entire installation won a Fountain of the Year award in 1995 but sadly you'll now need to resort to the internet to see the spectacle in full flow.

The installation often proved problematic and sprung leaks. Despite various renovations and repairs, in 2015 the water was turned off and the river bed became a flower bed instead.

It turns out the Floozie was tempting her dry fate from the day it was built. The sandstone perimeter of the Floozie's pool is engraved with lines from the poem 'Burnt Norton' by T.S.Eliot:

And the pool was filled with water of sunlight,
And the lotos rose, quietly, quietly,
The surface glittered out of heart of light,
And they were behind us, reflected in the pool.
Then a cloud passed, and the pool was empty.

Darn that passing cloud. An empty pool indeed. Thankfully, the council reported in 2019 that they had secured funding to restore the water feature back to its flowing splendour.

Footnote
Like Hoover, Onesie and Jet-Ski, Jacuzzi is a brand name/ trademark which has entered popular vocabulary as the everyday word for the item. You don't go up/ down a moving stairway but an Escalator and have a Jacuzzi in your hotel room (if you're lucky) not a heated, aerated bath tub The name is derived from the surname of two Italian brothers who founded the original company in Italy in 1915. The true pronunciation, and still is in Italian, would be 'yakutzzi' rather than the anglicised 'jackoozi'. Hence, the proper pronunciation doesn't even rhyme with Floozie. So there.

Chapter 5

A Tale of Two Plaques

Only a few of the people and places in this book have been endowed with a plaque. This chapter has two plaques and is the first demonstration that you can't always believe something just because it's been cast into a shiny metal disc on the wall.

Exhibit One

Is a brass plaque on the wall of 'The Actress and Bishop' pub on Ludgate Hill. It proudly proclaims this road was the site of the last public hanging in Birmingham. Mildly interesting you might think. Just the sort of thing to put on a plaque.

Exhibit Two

Less than half a mile's walk from Exhibit One is another plaque which also claims to be the site of the last public hanging in Birmingham. It is in a somewhat less salubrious location and is clinging onto to the wall with the aid of gaffer tape.

So which is right ?

Well, if appearance is anything to go by, you could be tempted to choose the gleaming and seemingly more recent brass plaque over the one held up with gaffer tape.

But I believe the gaffer tape, which also holds a clue that may have compelled the mounting of the erroneous brass plaque. The confusion seems to be that the last public hanging in the UK took place at Newgate prison near Ludgate Hill in London (not Birmingham).

So, if you're ever in the Actress and Bishop pub you might like to point out the error to the bar staff. I'm sure they'd be delighted to receive the feedback.

Footnote for completeness.
The last (non-public) hanging in Birmingham was of 20 year old Oswald Augustus Grey for the murder by shooting of a newsagent. The hanging took place in Winson Green prison on the morning of 20th November 1962.

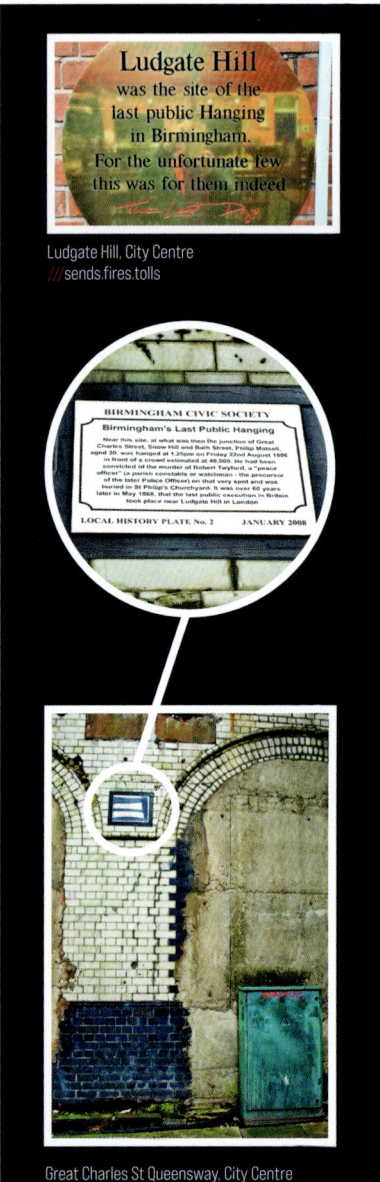

Ludgate Hill, City Centre
///sends.fires.tolls

Great Charles St Queensway, City Centre
///model.begun.having

22 | The Quirky Guide to Birmingham

Chapter 6

A Life in the Year of the Chinchillas

I guess that's the award for 'most unusual chapter title' in the bag. More about that later.

I've walked through Piccadilly Arcade countless times, whether to visit one of the independent, boutique shops or just as a pleasant cut through to New Street Station.

I had no idea about the arcade's history nor, evidently, did I bother to look skywards.

Piccadilly Arcade started life as a 'Picture House' in 1910 showing silent films. The conversion to a shopping arcade took place in 1926 but the floor still slopes like it did when there were once rows of seats.

You're in for a treat if you can avert your gaze from the window displays (or your phone) and look up. The length of the arcade's ceiling is covered in extraordinary works of art.

The series of murals were created in 1989 by the artist Paul Maxfield and symbolise the four seasons and human life cycle. If you're a bit Brian Sewell you might describe the murals as 'trompe l'oeil' (French for trick of the eye). You'd be wrong. A more accurate description is 'di sotto in su' which is Italian for 'from below upwards. It's a la-de-da way of saying it looks like the people in the pictures are peering down at you.

The skilful manipulation of perspective feels like you could jump up into the action or the parachuting man is about to land on your head.

Each time I look at the murals I seem to find some new detail or clandestine message that I hadn't noticed previously. Oh, and the reason for the particularly unusual chapter heading? That was the title Paul Maxfield gave to his artwork (but don't ask me why).

New Street, City Centre
///shows.trails.crown

The Quirky Guide to Birmingham | 23

Chapter 7

Interchange

You can find a 'Spaghetti Junction' in many countries (Australia, Botswana, USA etc.) but the first complex road junction to be given this name was Birmingham's Gravelly Hill Interchange which opened in 1972. The Spaghetti Junction moniker was first coined in an article in the local Birmingham Evening Mail.

In addition to the motorway network with 18 possible routes on six different levels there is a confluence of two rivers, a junction of three canals and two railway lines. All of which had to be modified or diverted in some way to allow construction of the interchange. As if that wasn't complicated enough, the placement of more than 500 concrete columns had to be carefully planned so that canal barges could still be pulled by horses without getting the ropes tangled up.

One of the pedestrian subway entrances to underneath Spaghetti Junction at Salford Circus.
Copeley Hill
///income.envy.aware

Spaghetti Junction is the most complicated road interchange in the UK. It's one of those places where being on it doesn't really afford full appreciation of the complexity and size. That's probably why most photos of it are taken from above.
However, there is another impressive view of the structure – from underneath. One of the easiest places to view Spaghetti Junction from below is at Salford Circus. A network of pedestrian subways congregate under the island (roundabout) here. Hundreds of thousands of vehicles pass through Spaghetti Junction every day but you'll see few people down here in the underbelly.

If you like concrete underneath big roads try page 80 too.

Below Salford Circus
///dads.jumpy.design

Chapter 8

Grave 36

Witton Cemetery opened in 1863 and is the largest cemetery in Birmingham. As kids we joked, badly, that it was the 'dead centre' of Birmingham. You'll see impressive monuments to some of the great and the good from Birmingham's history. But, as is often the case, some of the most incredible stories can be discovered in the most humble of places. In one corner of the cemetery you'll find a well-tended grass quadrangle with a series of modest, flat flagstones set into the turf. Beneath the stone simply engraved '36' is a common grave.

It is the last resting place of a man with a story as tragic as you could expect to find in the whole cemetery.

The Victoria Cross (VC) is the highest military award granted in Great Britain. Awards are scarce; in 164 years the medal has been awarded fewer than 1400 times. In the 75 years since the Second World War just 20 awards have been made. One of the requirements of award is that the recipient had a 90 per cent chance of being killed in action. VC recipients are a rare and highly distinguished group but there is an even rarer sub-set of VC winners. The ones that have had their medal taken away. Just eight 8 people in history have ever forfeited their VC. The last one ever lies in grave 36.

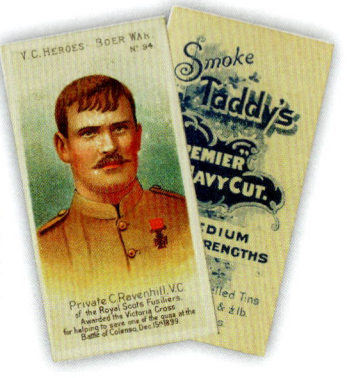

George Ravenhill
A 'Taddy' cigarette card issued ca. 1902 . Note that George is referred to as 'C' Ravenhill as his name appeared as Charles when he first joined the military.

George Albert Ravenhill was born in Birmingham in 1872 and spent much of his adult life in military service. He first joined the army at the age of 17 in 1889. He spent the first years of his career in overseas military campaigns including in India. In 1898 he was back in the UK and aged 26 he married Florence Langford. Their first child, Lily, was born in 1900, a few months after George had left for South Africa to fight in the Second Boer War.

George was evidently a good soldier having been awarded the Kings Medal, Queens Medal and Distinguished Conduct Medal but the piece de la resistance was the VC. On 15th December 1899 the Boer War was in full swing and George, now 27, found himself at the Battle of Colenso where he undertook the brave action which earnt him his VC. The citation for his VC reads: '…Private Ravenhill went several times, under a heavy fire, from his sheltered position as one of the escort to the guns, to assist the officers and drivers who were trying to withdraw the guns of the 14th and 66th Batteries, Royal Field Artillery, when the detachments serving them had all been killed, wounded, or driven from them by infantry fire at close range, and helped to limber up one of the guns that were saved'

George was shot and wounded during his courageous act but survived. He remained in South Africa to continue fighting in the war but in later action was captured and made a prisoner of war.

George was released in 1900 and in 1901, whilst still in South Africa, he was presented with his VC by The Duke of York.

The Second Boer War ended in 1902 and George returned to the UK the same

26 | The Quirky Guide to Birmingham

year. He was discharged from the army 13 years to the day that he first joined up. It was to prove an unlucky omen for George.

Back in Civvy Street, George and his family fell upon hard times. Really hard times. By 1906 George and Florence had two more children (George and Raymond) and, unable to support themselves, the entire family entered the workhouse.

Whilst in the workhouse George was charged with refusing to perform his allotted task. It seems this was simply a protest by George and in court he raised the issue that he was entitled to a pension of £50 per year and he would not find himself in his current conditions if he had received the pension.

The predicament of George as a VC winner had not gone unnoticed and some prominent politicians endeavoured to fight his corner. On at least two occasions in 1908 George's plight in the workhouse was raised in the House of Commons. But it was to no avail. By now there was another mouth to feed, Florence, and in August 1908 George was found guilty of stealing 30 shillings worth of scrap metal. He once again protested that he was entitled to a £50 pension which he had not received. He was unable to pay the 10 shillings fine so was imprisoned for a month.

Prison would not be the end of George's worries. The award of the VC had always included a condition that 'if any person on whom such distinction shall be conferred, be convicted of treason, cowardice, felony or of any infamous crime … his name shall forthwith be erased from the registry'.

And so, for the sake of some scrap metal, George's hopes of receiving his oft protested pension were dealt a final blow. The pension is forfeited as well as the medal.

If the authorities were slow to react to George's previous protests and his eligibility for a pension, they had found the impetus to react swiftly to his conviction. It appears the War Office confiscated all three of his medals including his VC. Within four months of his conviction his medals were sold at a Sotheby's auction for £42. To add insult to injury the date of the auction was nine years to the day that he risked his life to earn a VC.

Tragically, life was not about to take a turn for the better for George and his family. He and Florence had another child, Alfred, who died in his first year. In 1911 the family were again in the workhouse. Whilst there, their first three children were sent to Canada for fostering, leaving George and Florence with just their youngest surviving child, Florence, now aged 4. Heartbreak came again in 1912 when another family addition, Nellie, also died in her first year.

Despite everything that George had endured, with the outbreak of the First World War in 1914 his patriotism took over and he re-enlisted in the army once again aged 42. He saw active service in the Balkans before being discharged on health grounds in 1916. He was awarded the three WWI campaign medals, affectionately known as Pip, Squeak and Wilfred.

George and Florence had three more children, Arthur, William and Laura. In 1921 the couple and all their remaining children, now aged 2 to 14, lived together in Nechells, the same area where George was born. They were destitute and living in a one room, squalid tenement. George died of a heart attack on 14th April 1921 aged 49.

It is difficult to comprehend the misery George and his family must have suffered. Fighting for King and country all over the world, risking his life, shot, prisoner of war, workhouse, prison, denied a pension, medals taken away, watched two children die and three others sent away never to be seen again. Hopefully, death had brought a final peace for George but also, thankfully, it prompted some amends.

Upon George's death, his story and the family's plight quickly came to the public consciousness. Various campaigns took place to help ensure his family could live in better conditions and that George had the funeral he deserved.

George was buried with full military honours and the cost of his funeral was settled by the Mayor of Birmingham. A crowd assembled at his home. His coffin was borne on a gun carriage and draped with the Union Jack. Floral tributes covered the coffin including one from his regiment in the form of the Victoria Cross. His funeral cortège was headed by soldiers with arms reversed and accompanied by a military band. The procession made its way slowly to Witton Cemetery and large crowds had assembled to honour George. As he was laid to rest in grave 36 three volleys were fired and the last post played. Even the date was significant - this all took place on 23rd April 1921. St George's Day.

The man who presented George with his VC 20 years earlier was now King George V (grandfather of Queen Elizabeth II). The King expressed his clear view to the War Office against forfeiture of the Victoria Cross and that 'even if a man is convicted of murder he should be able to wear his VC at the gallows'. No VC has been forfeited since the King expressed his views but it was too late for George Ravenhill.

Grave 36
The quadrangle and marker of the last resting place of George Ravenhill in Witton Cemetery.
///roof.breath.change

Several organisations came to the aid of George's family and a concert was to be held in May 1921 to raise funds. Newspapers reported Florence's thanks for all the expressions of sympathy received and to those that had 'persevered to make my sad case known'.

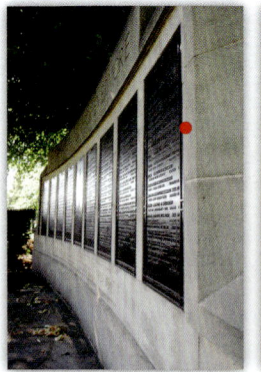

Memorial Screen Wall at Witton Cemetery
Listing the servicemen interred at the site. George Ravenhill's entry is marked with a red dot.
///rent.unions.skips

28 | The Quirky Guide to Birmingham

George's VC and other medals were eventually reunited with his regiment and are on display at the Royal Highland Fusiliers Museum in Glasgow.

Despite the pomp of George's funeral, his name on the bronze screen walls at Witton Cemetery did not recognise his VC. He would have to wait more than 80 years for 'VC' to be added to his name on the list. If you look closely you can tell that his inscription has been altered.

Whilst George was the last person to forfeit a VC, the possibility of forfeiture remains to this day, regardless of the expressed views of King George V. The current Queen has refused requests to reinstate another forfeited VC.

If you ever find yourself near Witton Cemetery, perhaps grab a couple of flowers from the sellers at the Moor Lane entrance and take them the short stroll to place on grave 36 to remember George Albert Ravenhill. VC.

Chapter 9

Will of the People

Somewhere in Birmingham an iron mountain holds a secret.

Say it in a deep voice and it could be the tag line to a new film about a dystopian future.

Instead, Iron Mountain 'is a global business dedicated to storing, protecting and managing, information and assets'. The business has a number of large repositories in the Birmingham area. Whoop de doo you might well say. But one of the storage facilities is a little special. Unique even.

I was surprised to learn that every 'Last Will and Testament' left by anyone in England and Wales is a matter of public record and anyone can ask to view them once they have passed through probate. Literally anyone – you don't need to be a family member or have special authority. That means every will has to be catalogued, stored, accessible and kept forever. And they are all stored in an Iron Mountain facility in Birmingham on behalf of the Government's Probate Service. That's all 41 million wills which have been left since 1858 and the number grows by around 250.000 every year.

There are some well known names amongst the wills because no matter how famous, rich, important or royal someone was, their will is still up for public scrutiny and stored in this facility.

Like who?
Diana, Princess of Wales? Tick.
Winston Churchill? Tick.
John Lennon, Charles Darwin and Beatrix Potter? Tick, tick,tick.
In fact most of the influential people of the 19th and 20th century as well as Joe Public, your own ancestors and neighbours.

Iron Mountain don't specify the exact location of the facility but it took me about ten minutes to find it having watched their own promotional video. Nonetheless, I haven't divulged the exact location. Just in case.

Even if you can locate the storage facility I wouldn't recommend turning up unannounced demanding to see Beatrix Potter's last will and testament. I'm pretty sure you won't get very far.

Instead, to view Beatrix's will, or just the one of your sadly missed next door neighbour, you can visit the official UK Government website (charges may apply): www.gov.uk/search-will-probate

30 | The Quirky Guide to Birmingham

Chapter 10

Nose

The piece of public art shown in the large photo below is called 'Sleeping Iron Giant'. The sculpture was made in 1992 by Ondre Nowakowski and described (on Wikipedia) as 'a metaphor for a site with an historic background of manufacturing industry'.

It is constructed from sintered iron and polyester resin mounted on a steel reinforced frame. You could add to the list a splash of blue gloss paint from the local hardware store (probably).

You can't help but notice that the sculpture's nose is blue. This was not an original design feature of the aforementioned artist. Let's say it was a secondary embellishment bestowed upon the sculpture, free of charge, by local artisans and is regularly kept in this condition. For the sake of balance others consider it vandalism.

Nearby this spot is the Birmingham City FC stadium and fans of that team have the nickname of 'Bluenoses'. It seemed apt that the big head should have a blue nose being so close to the football ground. At first the authorities tried to remove the paint but eventually gave up. The 'artists' were just more persistent.

This is not the only example of art being 'enhanced' by the public. A bust of Sir Josiah Mason in the centre of an island (roundabout) on Chester Road in Erdington can regularly be found in various forms of decoration to suit the time of year or events. These include Aston Villa garb, Irish flags (St. Patrick's Day), tinsel and even being 'yarn-bombed' with various red, white and blue crocheted garments in celebration of the Diamond Jubilee.

Garrison Lane
Bordesley Green
///cheat.danger.cling

///ocean.flash.meals

The Quirky Guide to Birmingham | 31

Chapter 11

Defenestration

It's the 1970s. Steve Austin is a man barely alive, The Clangers are unintelligible (see page 48) and pop stars are throwing TVs out of hotel windows on a regular basis. Usually Keith Moon from The Rolling Stones.

You don't really hear much about TV defenestration any more, especially in Birmingham.

In fact, the only report I could find of a pop star throwing a TV out of a Birmingham hotel window was Matt Willis from Busted (who is married to Brummie TV presenter Emma Willis).

Therefore, it came as quite a surprise to learn that a Birmingham window holds the record for having the most televisions thrown out of it; more than sixty of them. But don't expect to look up at the Hyatt Hotel and see a permanently boarded window. The story is slightly less rock 'n' roll.

On 19th January 2007 local radio station Kerrang! set the new record live on air by throwing 61 televisions out of a second story window in three minutes. The building in Digbeth was unused at the time and most of the televisions landed in a strategically placed skip below.

The window that's had more TVs thrown out of it than any other
Digbeth
///bells.wiser.half

32 | The Quirky Guide to Birmingham

Chapter 12

Brumyanmarvellous

The Shwedagon Pagoda is a spectacle to behold and vying for UNESCO World Heritage status. The central spire, or stupa, is way taller than the Rotunda, completely covered in real gold and capped with masses of precious gems. You may wonder how you have missed this marvel from the Birmingham skyline. Don't worry, you haven't. It's in Yangon, Myanmar (previously Rangoon, Burma).

However, in Ladywood there is a bijoux recreation of the Shwedagon Pagoda. It's not quite as big as the original but is still an impressive sight for a Brum side street. The Dhamma Talaka Pagoda is the only on of its kind in the UK and was opened in 1998. Its name means 'Reservoir of the Teaching', taking its cue from the reservoir of E. Coli (Edgbaston Reservoir) which sits behind the pagoda grounds. There is also a Buddhist monastery and academy on the site. Buddha relics from the former Burmese royal family are enshrined in the pagoda as is a chunk of the Berlin Wall, the reason for which I have not ascertained.

The Shwedagon Pagoda apparently has a 72 carat diamond adorning its peak. I'm guessing there's nothing similar atop the Brum pagoda unless it's really well insured.

Osler Street
Ladywood
A fitting 3 word address:
///chef.gold.shade

Chapter 13

JFK

I often pondered why there is a mosaic mural of John Fitzgerald Kennedy (JFK) in Birmingham and what provoked the choice of location. It's a long story. Well, just less than a page.

JFK was the first President of the USA with direct Irish heritage as well as being the only Roman Catholic president. He was assassinated in 1963.

To commemorate JFK the first mosaic was installed in 1968 in a pedestrian underpass near Birmingham's Roman Catholic cathedral; St Chad's. British artist Kenneth Budd was commissioned by Birmingham's Irish community to design and create the artwork. Panels of the mosaic were made in Budd's studio in London before being assembled at St Chad's.

The mural remained there for almost 40 years and I, like many Brummies, would mostly have admired it from the top deck of a bus going around St Chad's Circus island (roundabout) as the mosaic couldn't be seen from normal ground level.

The road network at St Chad's was redeveloped in 2007 and the underpass removed. During the works the mosaic was partially destroyed but Budd's son, Oliver Budd, managed to personally save some key parts of the mosaic.

Years passed and Oliver Budd was commissioned to recreate the mural in the current location in the city's Irish quarter where he commenced work in 2012. Like the original, the recreation benefited from funding from the Irish community.

Unfortunately, the original panels which Oliver Budd had salvaged could not be used due to colour differences so the new mosaic had to be made from scratch using the original designs. More than 200,000 individual tiles and 12 months later and the mural was unveiled. But it was not without some controversy.

Firstly, some complained that the date on the left side of the mosaic needed to be corrected. It shows JFK's presidency as starting in 1960 (when he won the election and became President Elect) and not when he was formally inaugurated as president in 1961. The original mural showed 1960 for decades.

Secondly, faces in the mosaic were the same as the original including depictions of Martin Luther King Jr. and Edward Kennedy. But a new face also appeared. This was Mike Nangle, the first Irish Lord Mayor of Birmingham who died in 2010. Nangle was a widely respected local councillor and member of the Irish community but opinion was divided on whether he should have been included in the mural.

Jackie Kennedy and children | Martin Luther King Jr. | Celtic Cross | Edward 'Ted' Kennedy | The White House | The Seal of the President of the United States | Mike Nangle Lord Mayor of Birmingham 2004/5

A MAN MAY DIE, NATIONS MAY RISE AND FALL, BUT AN IDEA LIVES ON

Floodgate St. Digbeth
///commented.puddles.grand

Chapter 14

Post

You may have heard the legend that you're never more than six feet away from a rat. An altogether less disturbing fact is that nearly every household in the UK is never more than half a mile from a pillar box.

A pillar box is a pillar box, right ? Well, not if you're a fan of this particular strain of street furniture. Some pillar boxes are much more interesting than others. Intrepid enthusiasts have been known to travel the length of the country to see the really rare ones.

In Birmingham there are a few of some of the rarest types (a couple of them can be seen in the photos on the opposite page). At first glance there is nothing obvious to make them special but you need to look a little closer. Observe the royal initials (cipher) on the front of the pillar boxes. It says 'ER VIII' which is the cipher for Edward VIII.

The Old Central Post Office
The post office here once had the prestigious post code of B1 1AA. A similar picture of the building can be found in UK passports issued after late 2015
Victoria Square
///owner.wooden.ritual

Edward VIII became King on 20th January 1936 but abdicated after just 326 days and before a coronation had taken place. This made Edward one of the shortest reigning monarchs in British history. Consequently, there are only a comparatively small number of post boxes that exist with his cipher.

The holy grail for pillar box enthusiasts is a small 'Ludlow' wall box with Edward VIII's cipher. These post boxes are smaller and usually set into walls. Only a handful are known to still exist in the whole of the UK. There are none known in Birmingham despite being manufactured here (Ludlow refers to the name of the manufacturer not the location).

Other rare pillar boxes are the hundred or so that were painted gold to commemorate the British gold medal winners at the 2012 Summer Olympics and Paralympics. Sadly, there are none of those in Birmingham but there is a pillar box which commemorates a local Victoria Cross winner, Sergeant Alfred Joseph Knight VC, who was also a postal worker (see photos above and right).

Pillar boxes only exist because of the invention of the postage stamp. Rowland Hill has strong connections with Birmingham and is widely recognised as being responsible for the introduction of the first postage stamp, the Penny Black, in 1840.

Hill St in the City Centre is not named because of the incline but in honour of Rowland Hill. There is still a Post Office on Hill Street but it is a far cry from the original, large Central Post Office at the top of Hill Street near Victoria Square.

///drain.librarian.lots

36 | The Quirky Guide to Birmingham

Pillar box with rare Edward VIII cipher

Digbeth
///tube.joins.fleet

Pillar box commemorating Victoria Cross recipient, Alfred Knight

Tennant Street, Five Ways
///shower.manual.dare

Another pillar box with rare Edward VIII cipher

Clay Lane, Yardley
///truly.bake.claps

An unusually positioned pillar box in a driveway

Let's just say the pillar box has been there for a hundred years or more and the gates and block paving are more recent. Birmingham City Council were reported as investigating 'unauthorised works'.
School Road, Moseley
///hill.neat.hints

The Quirky Guide to Birmingham | 37

Chapter 15
A Very Buried Man

A Brum creation from almost 300 years ago has transcended time and technology to be used more today than the man responsible ever imagined. His name is one of the most recognisable to come from Brum and can be found on virtually every computer.

This is a tale of flouting convention, genius, perseverance, flamboyance, industrial espionage, adultery, a curse and being buried three times including once standing up. Under a windmill.

John Baskerville once described himself as 'an early admirer of the beauty of letters'. He was born in 1706 in Worcestershire and in his teens developed an interest and skill in the art of writing. By his early twenties he had moved to Birmingham and was teaching as a 'Writing Master'. His calligraphic skills progressed to the engraving and design of epitaphs and gravestones. An elaborately engraved slate can still be found at The Library of Birmingham and says 'Grave Stones cut in any of the Hands by John Baskervill[1], Writing Master'. It is the only known remaining piece of his engraved work.

Baskerville House
Stands approximately on the original site of, well, Baskerville's house (Easy Hill).
Centenary Square
///piano.aspect.vibrates

Baskerville was not content with his lot. He wanted money. He observed a businessman, John Taylor, move to Birmingham and become rich from the art of japanning (an ornate form of decorating items which resembles oriental, black lacquer work). Armed with his artistic talents, Baskerville set upon getting a slice of that lucrative, lacquered pie. He taught himself japanning but it may not have been all his own work. Baskerville apparently resorted to following John Taylor to his various suppliers, bought the same materials and worked out the secret to the japanning process. Whatever he did, it worked. Now in his early 30s, Baskerville patented his process and built up a successful japanning business. In a few years it made him rich.

Baskerville wasn't shy about his wealth. He dressed flamboyantly with extravagant amounts of gold embellishments. He indulged his ample resources for gaudy decoration on his regular transport. Akin to an 18th century equivalent of today's Lamborghini with a flash paint job going down Broad Street making sure everyone knows it has a loud exhaust, Baskerville's coach was bestowed with ostentatious japanning and drawn by light coloured horses. Naturally, he needed a nice new pad to park his wheels and reflect his substance. He ended up spending today's equivalent of £1.3 million developing the original Baskerville House, 'Easy Hill', an idyllic home and gardens on the (back then) leafy outskirts of Birmingham. The sprawling eight acres included stables, servant

Baskerville's Chariot
This cigratte card from ca. 1932 may have used significant artistic licence in the dipiction of Baskerville's ostentatious coach.

1   Baskerville added the 'e' to the end of his name later when he became more, well, posh.

38 | The Quirky Guide to Birmingham

quarters, coach house, warehouses, workshops, fish ponds, a grotto and even a choice of water supplies.

Baskerville's flamboyancy was matched by his irreverence and unorthodoxy. He didn't tone down his colourful apparel even when attending a funeral, was contemptuous of religion and had an enduring adulterous relationship. Strong stuff for the 18th century, even for relatively broad-minded Birmingham.

In his early 40s Baskerville took in Sarah Eaves and her three children after her husband, Richard, became a fugitive of justice. This apparent act of charity may have been as a favour to a relative of Sarah who was a supporter of Baskerville. Sarah was initially a housekeeper but the relationship became overtly much more and Sarah was to all intents 'Mrs Baskerville'. This status became official in 1764 when Sarah and John were married within weeks of the death of Richard Eaves.

Aged around 50 Baskerville returned to his first love of letters and set about publishing books. He didn't do things by halves. Baskerville went on to not only painstakingly design the font that took his name but also perfect the paper, press and even the ink. Seven years would pass before his first book was published in 1757. More than 50 other titles would follow.

Spot the Baskerville

The Baskerville typeface is widely used but you might not notice it. Here are some tell tale signs of the most Brummie of fonts.

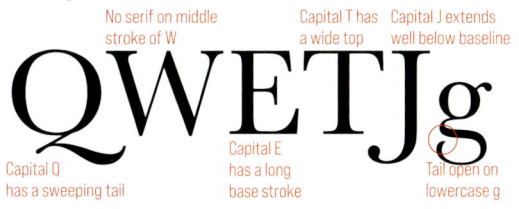

- No serif on middle stroke of W
- Capital T has a wide top
- Capital J extends well below baseline
- Capital Q has a sweeping tail
- Capital E has a long base stroke
- Tail open on lowercase g

QWETJg

Baskerville had sparked a mini revolution in printing. In contradiction to Baskerville's vibrant life, simplicity and clarity were the principles for his books. They had an airy feel with larger line spacings, wider margins and little decorative embellishment. Elegant, sharp lettering in rich, black ink on glossy paper completed the style which 'went forth to astonish the librarians of Europe' or cause one biographer to proclaim Baskerville 'the greatest printer that England has ever produced'. Ironically, for someone who had little good to say of religion, Baskerville saved his finest work for printing a Bible.

Baskerville died in 1775 in his 69th year. Given his disdain of religion and that he was once an engraver of headstones, he naturally made careful preparations for his death.

Baskerville was particularly keen to not be buried in, what he described as, 'the farce of a consecrated ground'. He directed that his resting place would be in the grounds of his home at Easy Hill. His oak coffin was encased in lead and placed upright in a vault beneath a conical shaped building which he had specially prepared and adapted from a windmill. The finishing touch was the epitaph which he penned himself and would serve as enduring testimony to his scathing opinions:

Stranger –

Beneath this Cone in unconsecrated ground
A friend to the liberties of mankind directed his body to be inhum'd.
May the example contribute to emancipate thy mind
From the idle fears of superstition
And the wicked arts of Priesthood.

Sarah Baskerville continued with parts of the business and printed further books but she eventually sold the printing business. Baskerville's printing punches went to France with a multi-talented Frenchman with the highfalutin name of Pierre-Augustin Caron de Beaumarchais.

Perhaps Baskerville would have been pleased that Beaumarchais used the letter punches to publish works of Voltaire which were banned in France. Maybe less pleased that his beloved punches were later rumoured to have been melted down to make arms for the French Revolution.

Sarah outlived Baskerville by 13 years and died in 1788. Their home at Easy Hill was sold complete with Mr Baskerville. In 1996 font designer Zuzana Licko ensured that Sarah was also immortalised in a font of her own. She named the Baskerville inspired font Mrs Eaves.

Conventional life stories might end there. Instead, there would be another 200 years of posthumous excitement for Mr B.

All the clues are that Baskerville did not believe in the afterlife, but legend has it that on his death bed he indicated that if resurrection was a thing then he would return in fifty years. As fake predictions go, it wasn't a bad effort.

Baskerville's peace was first disturbed 16 years after his death in 1791. During the 'Priestly Riots' Easy Hill was a target of arson and largely destroyed, but Baskerville remained in his vault.

The estate agent's blurb for Easy Hill had described it as 'a very desirable spot to build upon'. They hadn't exaggerated. As Birmingham grew, the Easy Hill land was developed for canals and wharves. Baskerville was dug up during works and his coffin opened in 1821, 46 years after his death. Press accounts of the opening reported that he was remarkably well preserved. However, a strong smell of rotting cheese led to the cover being hastily replaced. The coffin spent the next eight years or so gathering dust in a warehouse belonging to the land developer, Mr Gibson. In 1829 Gibson transferred the coffin to Job Marston, Plumber and Glazier.

Now, it may just be a coincidence but in life Baskerville was familiar with the name Marston. Baskerville bequeathed money to various Marstons, his niece having married into that family. Was it this connection which caused Baskerville to be moved to Job Marston or did the coffin just need a new lid? Did the Marston's have some grudge against Baskerville which caused them to expose his corpse to anyone that was prepared to pay a miserly fee? True or not, it does seem clear that Baskerville's body was subjected to more scrutiny than was dignified whilst in Marston's custody. Someone took a cast of Baskerville's head, a rather ghoulish sketch was made of his remains, claims were made of teeth and clothing being purloined. Various pieces of the shroud were pocketed, including by a Brum surgeon who dropped dead a few days later. The sketch and a piece of the shroud are kept at The Library of Birmingham which still reports that you will be cursed if you touch the small piece of cloth. I hope someone is keeping an eye on the mortality statistics of librarians.

Whether motivated by diminishing public interest, intervention of the authorities, outrage of Baskerville fans, fear of illness or just the smell, Marston needed to be rid of Mr B. It would not be straightforward given Baskerville's beliefs, or lack of. For example, requests to have him buried with his wife in the consecrated ground of St Philip's Cathedral were declined.

Nonetheless, Marston appeared to have found a solution and in September 1829 newspapers reported that Baskerville had been re-buried in ground adjoining Cradley Chapel which had links to the Baskerville family. Phew.

Over the next 60 years gossip and stories surfaced which heaped doubt on the report of Baskerville's body ever going to Cradley. It was rumoured to be in a Birmingham church.

The church warden at Christ Church in Birmingham city centre made some checks and discovered that there was indeed a body where a body ought not be. Suspect vault 521 beneath the church had been sealed in an unconventional manner and bore no inscription. Were the rumours true?

On 12th April 1893 more than 20 people, including the Mayor, Coroner, Medical Officer, Chief Constable and journalists, gathered outside vault 521. Their subsequent actions would raise questions in parliament and risk imprisonment, but ultimately no legal action was taken. A Mr Timmins recounted Baskerville's story that had led to this point and described him as 'a very buried man'. The vault wall was demolished to reveal a leaden coffin with the name 'John Baskerville' spelled out using actual, if slightly shonky, pieces of his own typeface. The dignitaries satisfied themselves that it was indeed Baskerville, sealed him back in his coffin and bricked up the vault. A new plaque was placed at Christ Church proudly declaring the resting place of the famous Birmingham printer.

Remnants of Christ Church
The one time resting place of Baskerville, Christ Church, has long gone but some remnants persist. Christchurch Passage is little more than a staircase at the east side of Victoria Square. The drinking fountain which now stands on the southern limits of St Philip's churchyard (Pigeon Park) was originally at Christ Church.
Christchurch Passage: ///wisdom.jazz.bench
Drinking Fountain: ///itself.mercy.goals

In turns out that back in 1829 Marston had embarked upon a cunning plan. Marston schemed with a previous church warden of Christ Church, and possibly the vault owner, to place Baskerville in an empty vault at Christ Church. Marston appropriated the keys to the Christ Church catacombs in a classic case of plausible deniability by the church warden. Baskerville's coffin was taken to the vault in little more than a wheelbarrow. The press announcement of Baskerville's burial miles away in Cradley was, perhaps, the finishing touch to the deception. Once again, Baskerville was only in transit at Christ Church. The building was demolished in 1898, just 5 years after Baskerville was discovered there. In the same year Baskerville found his current resting place. He was re-re interred beneath the chapel of Warstone Lane Cemetery. Yet still his peace was disturbed. The chapel above him was demolished in the 1950s.

Though the chapel was gone, Baskerville still lies in a vault but there is no ground level identification of whom lies below. Thankfully, parts of Warstone Lane are being renovated including the area where the chapel once stood. It is planned to mark once again the resting place of one of Birmingham's biggest names

Whilst Baskerville was on his tour of Birmingham graveyards

Finally at Rest ?
Renovation works are underway (September 2020) on the site of the old chapel which once stood over Baskerville at Warstone Lane Cemetery. When completed the resting place of Baskerville will be marked once again for the first time in decades.
Warstone Lane Cemetery.
///flags.heads.onions

The Quirky Guide to Birmingham | 41

his beloved typeface fell into obscurity in Britain. Despite the many plaudits of Baskerville's publishing output there was not universal acclaim and it was not a financial success. One dissenter proclaimed that Baskerville's books would cause the nation to go blind. Thankfully, the rumours that Baskerville's letter punches had been destroyed during the French Revolution were unfounded and thus his typeface continued being used more on the continent than in Britain. It wasn't until the beginning of the 20th century that the Baskerville font found resurgence in Britain and grew to the international omnipresence of today. In 1953 Baskerville's original punches came home. Almost. In an act of benevolence by the French owners, Baskerville's punches were gifted to Cambridge University Press for whom Baskerville had printed many books.

There is a fitting tribute to Baskerville just in front of the main entrance to Baskerville House in Centenary Square. A greater honour, of course, is that the main text of this book is set in a Baskerville font. I didn't want to risk Baskerville turning in his grave. Again.

Baskerville Memorial
Baskerville's first publication was the works of Roman poet, Virgil in 1757.
Centenary Square
///snack.divisions.device

Hounds

Alright, let's cut to the chase. What you really want to know is whether the Sherlock Holmes story 'The Hound of the Baskervilles' has anything to do with Baskerville House or John Baskerville. Surprisingly, the answer, quite possibly, is yes.

Sherlock Holmes creator Sir Arthur Conan Doyle lived in Aston for a while between 1879 and 1882 whilst working in a pharmacy. The inspiration for the novel may well have come during that time.
///spoken.with.sits

42 | The Quirky Guide to Birmingham

Chapter 16

Getting an 'OO'*

Britain has the third highest per person consumption of tea in the world (Turkey and Ireland are first and second respectively). The phrase 'putting the kettle on' is peculiar to Britain; you'll seldom hear it in any other nation. Similarly, packing tea bags in your suitcase and experiencing a moment of panic upon entering a hotel room to find there is no kettle are also typically British traits.

The kettle, therefore, is a vital piece of kit for a tea making nation. It is particular to tea because tea needs near boiling water† to make a brew whereas coffee can be made in a pan whilst the water gradually heats up.

The essential electric kettles we use at home today are largely thanks to forerunners made in Birmingham. The first submersible electric heating element was invented by Bulpitt & Sons in 1922 at their factory on Camden Street. This innovation allowed a comparatively large amount of water to be boiled quickly. However, the kettle still had the risk of boiling dry and causing fires. Bulpitt later created a safety improvement to automatically disconnect the power if the element overheated.

Bulpitt manufactured their kettles and other appliances at the Birmingham factory under the 'Swan' brand. You can still buy a Swan branded kettle today but, alas, they are no longer manufactured in Birmingham or, indeed, the UK. In fact, a quick search found it was impossible to buy a new domestic electric kettle that is made in the UK. Surprising given the affinity Brits have for the appliance.

The last manufacturing at Camden Street was in 2006 and the factory was re-developed into luxury apartments called, naturally, The Kettleworks.

*'You only get an 'OO' with Typhoo was an advertising slogan of Typhoo Tea. The brand was founded in Birmingham in 1903 and manufactured tea products at their factory in Digbeth until 1978.
†ISO 3103:2019 "Tea - Preparation of liquor for use in sensory tests" published by the International Organization for Standardization can provide further guidance. No, I haven't made that up.

The Quirky Guide to Birmingham | 43

Chapter 17

Sentinel

There is a place in Birmingham where some of the homes may once have had a Spitfire parked where the kitchen is now. Or, maybe, a runway under the living room. I'll avoid the temptation for cheap jokes about leaving the landing light on. Oh, too late.

The Castle Vale estate was built in the 1960s on the site of Castle Bromwich Aerodrome. Twenty years earlier this was one of the most important sites in the country for the efforts during World War II. Just across Chester Road, where the Jaguar factory is now, was the largest Spitfire factory in the world – Castle Bromwich Aircraft Factory. Over 12,000 Spitfires were produced here, more than anywhere else. Finished aircraft, which also included Lancaster bombers, would be towed from the factory, across Chester Road, to the aerodrome opposite and handed over to test pilots before being flown on to their new homes at bases around Britain.

Examples of the aeronautics inspired street names of Castle Vale.
It does seem a little insensitive to name a street a 'Walk' after a flying ace that had both legs amputated.
///labels.props.clean
///invent.flows.supply

Spitfire Island
If you've read page 14 you'll know that traffic roundabouts are often referred to as islands so naturally, this roundabout is know as 'Spitfire Island'. Unusually, it is also the official name which is shown on maps. There used to be street name signs on the island which are, erm, no longer present.
The official name of this sculpture is 'Sentinel'. It was made by metal sculptor Tim Tolkien who has a local workshop and is the great-nephew of J.R.R. Tolkien.
///speak.rubble.hoot

44 | The Quirky Guide to Birmingham

A Spitfire made at the factory used to be on display at the factory entrance but is now exhibited in Thinktank.

Apart from the magnificent Spitfire sculpture, there are other clues to the area's heritage. Many road names on the estate reference famous names from aeronautics. At the main entrance to the Jaguar factory you can still see the original gate posts complete with propeller emblems. Also, on the headers of some of the rainwater downpipes there are wing and roundel emblems.

Smaller signs of the aeronautical past of the Jaguar factory.
(Top) One of the original gate posts at the main entrance to the factory with five white propeller emblems on the lower half.
Chester Road
///fence.jolly.ledge
(Bottom) A winged roundel on a rainwater hopper at the top of the building.
Fort Parkway
///translated.lamp.globe

The Quirky Guide to Birmingham | 45

Chapter 18
Going Underground

Have you ever watched a James Bond film and wondered how on Earth the villain managed to build his massive, clandestine lair in a volcano (or rainforest etc.) without anyone even raising a Roger Moore eyebrow?

Well, maybe they just did what happened in Birmingham and lied about what was really being built. In the early 1950s we were well into the atomic age and the threat of nuclear annihilation (for which Birmingham can take some responsibility – see page 84) loomed large.

The government decided that the country needed some super-secret, super-important bomb proof communication hubs that would enable essential communications to continue in the event of a nuclear attack. One of the hubs was destined for Birmingham.

Construction was underway by 1953 and the official explanation for the massive amount of machinery and workers disappearing underground every day was that Birmingham was to have an underground rail system. People working on the project were sworn to secrecy and many may not have known the true purpose of their labours. Four years and £4 million (around £100 million today) later, construction was complete and the good people of Birmingham may have spotted that they still didn't have a nice new underground system. The explanation was that the system was no longer economically viable so no underground. Sorry.

The new creation was akin to a small, self-sufficient subterranean town called Anchor Exchange (see page 58 to understand the relevance of anchor). Cavernous tunnels up to 100ft (30m) below ground were made of thick concrete and full of switchgear and communication gubbins. The outside world could be sealed off behind huge blast doors. Anchor could rely upon its own power supply from underground generators, a dedicated water supply from a source even deeper underground, air filtering systems, kitchens, dormitory, mess room, offices and an obligatory snooker table. So at least you could enjoy a few frames whilst the population above was dying of radiation poisoning.

In 1962 the authorities which conceived Anchor must have felt smug as along came the Cuban Missile Crisis and Anchor was put on full alert. It was probably the only occasion.

As time went on, communications technology got smaller and nuclear bombs got bigger so Anchor was no longer fit for its original purpose. By 1968 the official veil of secrecy regarding the existence of Anchor was lifted and it became public knowledge.

The tunnels became largely defunct but started to be utilised as a conduit to lay more modern cabling in the city without digging up the roads. These days this artefact of the cold war is more at risk from the rising water table than nuclear attack.

The tunnels are not accessible to the public but occasional tours have been held. Above ground evidence of the tunnels can still be seen though, perhaps most prominent is a ventilation shaft (see map opposite) which can be seen from Great Charles Street Queensway.

Plaque Identifying Tunnels
Part of 'The Findings Trail', one of two Jewellery Quarter Trails (see page 86 for the other one).
Newhall Street
///plot.origin.sleeps

BRUM'S 'SECRET' TUNNELS

UNFINISHED TUNNEL ENDS UNDER QUEENS HEAD PUB

BT TOWER

VENTILATION TOWER

TUNNELS SHOWN IN PINK

TELEPHONE HOUSE

TUNNEL CONTINUES APPROX. 2 MILES TO EXCHANGE ON ESSEX STREET

Chapter 19

Acme

There are some things that are so taken for granted that it's difficult to imagine a time when they didn't exist. In early games of football the officials would gain attention by waving a handkerchief. The first time a whistle was used by match officials was in 1878; 15 years after the FA was formed. That first match whistle was thanks to Brum legend and whistle entrepreneur Joseph Hudson.

J Hudson and Co. has been producing whistles for 150 years. Their unassuming factory on Barr St is home to the largest whistle manufacturer in the world. They also produce the most famous whistles in the world. Since that first use in 1878 there is barely a sporting event that hasn't benefited from their whistles. From Sunday league to the World Cup, police forces and fire brigades the world over, Brum whistles have given faithful service to them all.

The Home of Acme Whistles
on Barr Street since 1909.
///tinsel.wool.until

If you're of a certain age and you see the word 'Acme' you'll probably be picturing Wile E Coyote with an implausible invention from Acme Co. trying to catch the Roadrunner. It inevitably ends with Mr Coyote as a cloud of dust in a deep ravine or with an Acme anvil on his head. Acme isn't just the stuff of cartoons - it's the real major brand name of whistles produced by J Hudson and Co. An Acme whistle never found itself in a Roadrunner cartoon but the 'Acme Slide Whistle' did provide the vocals for The Clangers and for The Simpsons' Sideshow Bob before he found his own voice (well, Kelsey Grammer's).

In addition to major sporting events and cartoon characters, Hudson's whistles have also witnessed some of the most tragic events in history.

If you can picture the final scene of 'Blackadder Goes Forth' as the troops go over the top of the First World War trenches, in real life it was Hudson's whistles that would have been blown to signal the advance.

An Acme Thunderer Whistle
More than 300 million have been sold worldwide.

Perhaps most famously though, Hudson's whistles were used on the Titanic. It is the shrill of an Acme Thunderer whistle which called passengers to the lifeboats as the ship went down.

Footnote.
J Hudson & Co was one of the first examples of using 'Acme' as a brand name but many other international companies have, and still do, use the name. This includes a real manufacturer of anvils. Acme is ancient Greek for pinnacle or peak. It also appears near the top of alphabetic telephone listings. It is thought that the combination of these factors originally led to the prolific use of 'Acme' by businesses.

Chapter 20

A Sunflower Among the Roses

If you wander around the historic streets of Sutton Coldfield you will see many roses (see page 68) but only one sunflower, regardless of the season.

The simple engraved plaque which accompanies this striking piece of public art states 'Helianthus, Nicola Dixon & John McKenna' giving no clue of how it came to be here.

Nicola Dixon studied Art and Photography at the local Fairfax School. Helianthus was one of her A Level designs. Nicola never saw her design realised in this bronze by sculptor John McKenna.

On New Year's Eve 1996 Nicola was raped and murdered. She was 17. Her body was found lying in the snow the following day near where the sunflower can be seen today. The sculpture, produced as a memorial to Nicola, was unveiled here in 2000 by her parents Rita and Andy Dixon. They would have to wait another three years before Nicola's killer was caught and jailed for life in 2003.

It was only by a twist of fate that Nicola was in Sutton Coldfield during New Year. Her family had gone to spend the festivities with friends in Northumberland but Nicola had stayed behind because she was due to take her driving test. She didn't take that test; it was cancelled due to the snow.

Chapter 21

Graffiti

It wasn't until 2019 that Birmingham got its first, bone-fide Banksy. The festive piece was revealed by Banksy on Instagram on 9th December 2019. His video showed an apparently homeless man lying on a bench with his bags of belongings beside him and the bench 'sleigh' being pulled by the painted reindeer. Banksy said 'God bless Birmingham. In the 20 minutes we filmed Ryan on this bench passers-by gave him a hot drink, two chocolate bars and a lighter - without him ever asking for anything.'

Naturally, within hours of the reveal someone thought they could 'improve' Banksy's efforts and sprayed a red nose on each reindeer. Even though everyone knows only one reindeer, Rudolph, has a red nose. Cue some hastily arranged, shonky plastic sheeting to protect the work. Subsequently, even the plastic covering was vandalised with minimal artistic intent. The covering was replaced and the defaced one auctioned off raising £2300 for a homeless charity.

Pre Banksy, Birmingham already had a vast amount of other striking street art/graffiti to admire. Much of it is centred around a few streets in Digbeth. A stroll or drive along any of the streets written in yellow on the map opposite will offer some stunning pieces. The works are constantly changing so you may not see the exact creations shown in this chapter but there is likely to be something equally spectacular in its place.

Rudolph the Red Nosed Reindeer
Had a very none-original-Banksy shiny nose.

Birmingham's Only Banksy
Vyse Street, Jewellery Quarter
///shins.branded.dollar

Covid-19 Mural
This dazzling mural is a little outside the area covered by the map below but is worthy of a special mention. The artist is Josh Billingham (AKA Gent 48) who titled the work 'Forward in Unity'. Multi-cultural Brummies and emergency services are depicted lining up to defeat the Covid-19 invader looming over the Birmingham skyline. The fightback is fronted by an individual astride 'The Guardian' bull (see Contents page) and brandishing the Birmingham Community Flag (see page 67). The mural is within the courtyard of Norton's Bar but can also be admired from the pavement outside.
Meriden Street, Digbeth
///exist.snap.prone

Gibb Street
Gets my nomination for the award of 'Street that looks most like it's not allowed to drive along but, actually, you can'.
///enjoy.rally.lofts

JFK MURAL
SEE PAGE 34

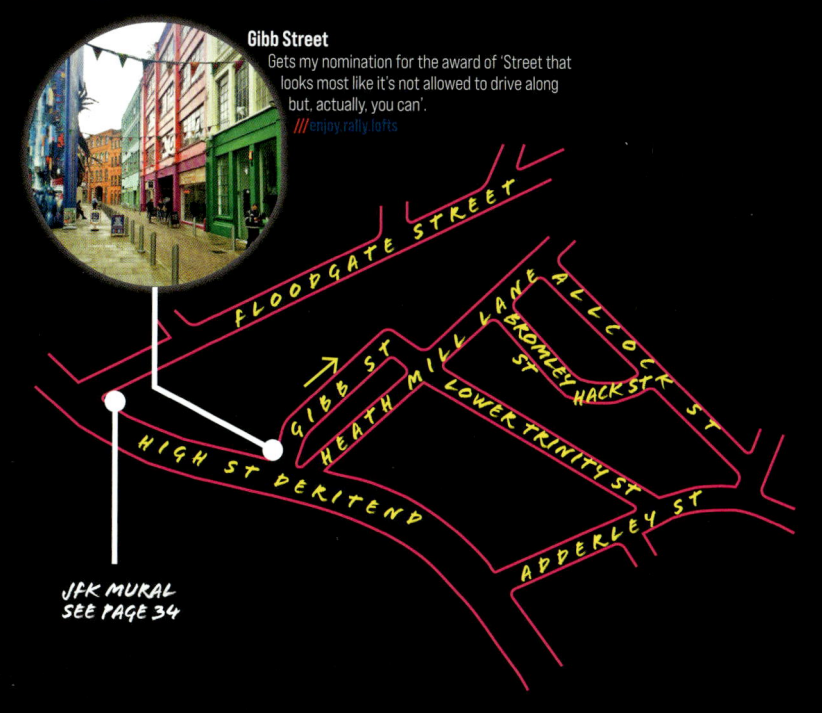

The Quirky Guide to Birmingham | 51

1. **Car park off High St Deritend,** /// aets.labs.voices
2. **Hack St,** /// deeres.ears.fortunate
3. **Adderley St,** /// rains.tunes.tape
4. **Hack St,** /// lace.broad.bill
5. **Adderley St,** /// drill.hunter.birds

52 | The Quirky Guide to Birmingham

6. **Lower Trinity St,** ///
7. **Lower Trinity St,** ///
8. **Hack St,** ///
9. **Allcock St,** ///
10. **Gibb St,** ///
11. **Gibb St,** ///

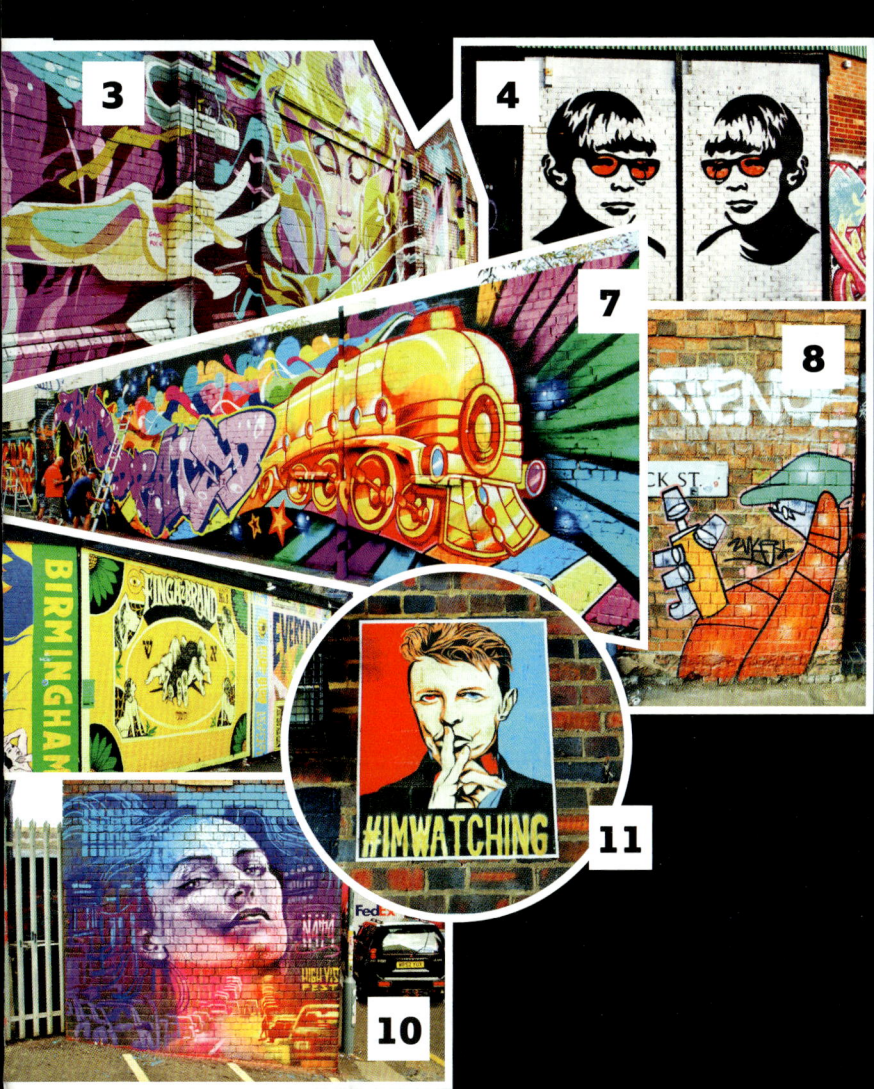

Chapter 22

Diamond Geezers

It should come as no surprise that Birmingham is the largest jewellery producer in the UK. The first diamond cut in Birmingham was a four carat whopper the 'Spencer Diamond'. It was named after the jeweller, William Spencer, who donated it to the city in 1873. The diamond was incorporated into the chains of office of the Lord Mayor of Birmingham.

Naturally, the historic and valuable gem was well looked after, but one spring day it was lost. And it was hanging around the Lord Mayor's neck at the time.

In the 1960s Cannon Hill Park started to hold a Tulip Festival. This annual event continued until the 1980s. It wasn't the kind of festival we are familiar with these days so put any images of a Brum Glastonbury out of your head. The park was transformed into an impressive sea of colourful blooms and associated events over several days in springtime (local personalities, vintage car rallies, you know the sort of thing).

It was customary for the Lord Mayor of Birmingham to perform the official opening of the event and on Saturday 17th May 1975 the honour fell to The Lord Mayor, Councillor E. James (Jim) Eames.

After doing his bit ceremony-ing in full regalia, the Lord Mayor returned to his chauffeur driven car and was undoubtedly horrified to find that the mahoosive diamond was missing from the elaborate gold chains of office he was wearing. An immediate, panicked search took place but to no avail. The diamond, said to worth around £100,000, was gone.

For years the whole thing was kept very low key and the council paid for a replacement diamond. Subsequent managers and staff at Cannon Hill Park were made aware of the loss in readiness for a find. In 2014 the Council went public and offered a reward of £20,000 for the gem's return but without success. The diamond still hasn't been recovered since the fateful day in 1975.

Doubtless Lord Mayor Eames was mortified by the mishap but, rightly, it does not seem he was otherwise penalised for the loss. He continued in public service, awarded an MBE and was widely respected for the way he responded as Lord Mayor in the aftermath of the Birmingham Pub Bombings. Jim Eames died in 2010 at the age of 92.

As the missing gem is still potentially in the park waiting to be found, I thought I'd summon up my inner Poirot and look for clues of where to look. Following an extensive, cursory, investigation of documents from the time of the loss, I endeavoured to retrace the steps of the Lord Mayor at the park and thus narrow down where the diamond may have dropped. The map opposite has been produced using details from the 1975 festival. The only thing that seems sure is that the Lord Mayor was due to perform the opening ceremony at the 'Golden Hind' at 2.45pm. Presumably his Mayoral transport was parked in the officials' car park but after that it's all pretty vague. Did he pop down for a carousel ride at the fun fair, grab a pint from the beer garden or watch a spot of wrestling? Who knows? I don't.

Good luck.

Footnote - Amazingly, this was not the first time the diamond was misplaced by a Lord Mayor. In 1938 the Lord Mayor, Councillor E. Canning, became separated from the diamond whilst he was attending a gala in Kingstanding. Thankfully a 13 year old girl found and returned the gem on that occassion.

YE OLDE TREASURE MAP OF CANNON HILL PARK*

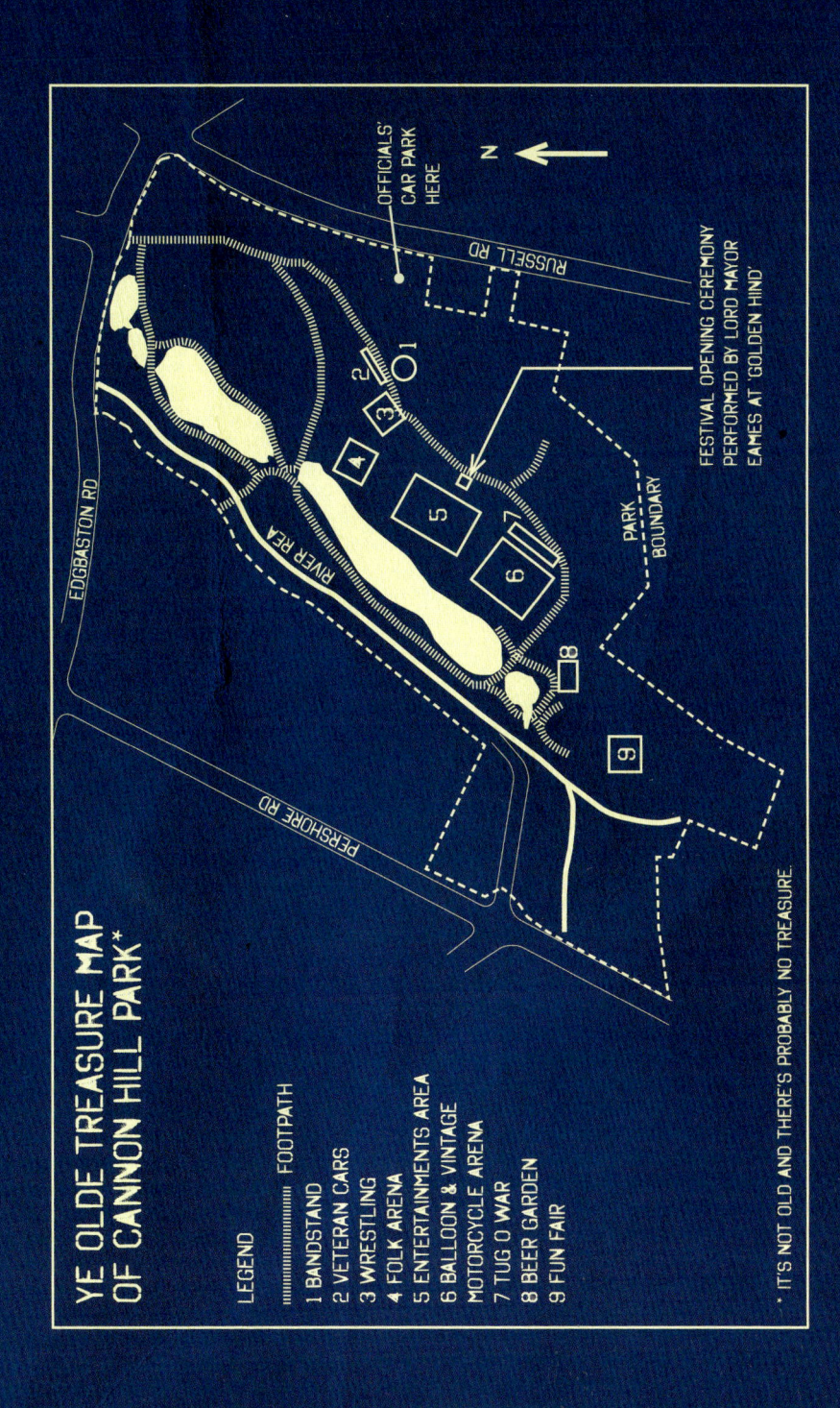

LEGEND

······· FOOTPATH

1 BANDSTAND
2 VETERAN CARS
3 WRESTLING
4 FOLK ARENA
5 ENTERTAINMENTS AREA
6 BALLOON & VINTAGE MOTORCYCLE ARENA
7 TUG O WAR
8 BEER GARDEN
9 FUN FAIR

OFFICIALS' CAR PARK HERE

FESTIVAL OPENING CEREMONY PERFORMED BY LORD MAYOR EAMES AT 'GOLDEN HIND'

PARK BOUNDARY

RUSSELL RD
EDGBASTON RD
PERSHORE RD
RIVER REA

* IT'S NOT OLD AND THERE'S PROBABLY NO TREASURE.

Chapter 23

Listed

In the same way that some people don't realise that Rice Krispies are actually made from rice, it can come as a surprise that buildings which are described as 'listed' do indeed appear on a list.

The full name of the list is 'The National Heritage List for England' and it's maintained by Historic England. The list originates from 1882 but the list as we know it today didn't really start until after the Second World War. In the words of Historic England 'listing marks and celebrates a building's special architectural and historic interest, and also brings it under the consideration of the planning system, so that it can be protected for future generations'.

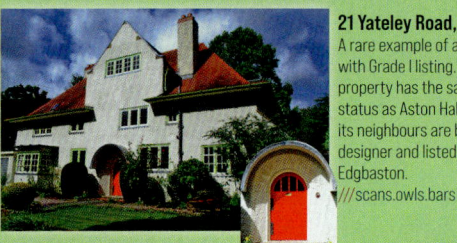

21 Yateley Road, Grade I
A rare example of a private home with Grade I listing. This beautiful property has the same listing status as Aston Hall. Many of its neighbours are by the same designer and listed too.
Edgbaston.
///scans.owls.bars

Wake Green Prefabs, Grade II
Temporary homes erected in the 1940s to last around 10 years. Still in use more than 70 years later. Wake Green Road, Moseley.
///period.drums.lower

Water Tower, Grade II
1905
Hollymore Hospital, Tessall Lane
///market.mostly.brave

Play Sculpture, Grade II
1960s by John Bridgeman. Is this the most disturbing children's play sculpture ever made ?
Curtis Gardens, Fox Hollies Road, Acocks Green
///silent.radio.fled

The Ohel, Grade II
Birmingham Hebrew Congregation Cemetery. Note the year designation over the entrance in Hebrew years and Georgian calender
Warren Road, Kingstanding.
///soon.survey.clash

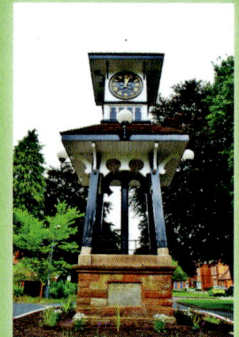

Clock Tower, Grade II
1898
Erdington Cottage Homes, The Gardens, Erdington.
///purple.rams.bats

56 | The Quirky Guide to Birmingham

There are three types of listed status for buildings in England and Wales: Grade I: buildings of exceptional interest. Grade II*: particularly important buildings of more than special interest and Grade II: buildings that are of special interest, warranting every effort to preserve them.

There are more than 1400 listed buildings, structures and ancient monuments in Birmingham. Just 22 are the highest Grade I. The obvious choices are there like Aston Hall, Town Hall, etc. but there is also a good selection of items that maybe you wouldn't expect like urinals, canal locks, street lamps, and statues.

Here is a quirky dozen which can all be viewed from public roads/ footpaths.

Bollard, Grade II
Yes, really; it's a bollard.
Frederick Road, Edgbaston
///news.puff.crunch

New Street Station Signal Box, Grade II
An example of Brutalist architecture from the 1960s. Still used to control all the train comings and goings at Britain's busiest station outside London.
Navigation Street, City Centre
///forms.ranch.ending

'Zig Zag' Bridge, Grade II
You could pass along the duel carriageway next to this bridge for years and not realise it was there. I did. About 300 years old.
Aldridge Road, Perry Barr
///hulk.backs.dollar

Former GEC Administration Block, Grade II
Art Deco style from 1922. Can be seen from the Aston Expressway.
Dulverton Road, Witton
///last.sits.remove

Telephone Boxes, Grade II
No longer functioning but can be rented for business use.
Eden Place, City Centre
///speech.sudden.counts

Block of Six Flats, Grade II
Arts and Crafts style built in 1908
Ravenhurst Rd, Moor Pool Estate
///librarian.share.maker

The Quirky Guide to Birmingham | 57

Chapter 24
Keeping it Real, Bab

Birmingham is well known for its Jewellery Quarter. Row upon row of shops with people pressed against the windows, transfixed by the shiny things inside. The vast majority of that shiny stuff will have one thing in common – at some point it would have passed through another Birmingham institution.

A (gem)stone's throw away from the shops is a large, somewhat uninspiring, blue brick building where you are unlikely to find anyone stood outside peering in. A large symbol of an anchor is emblazoned on the front of the building with the date 1773. However, this is not an anchor factory or a branch of the shipping company Kuehne + Nagel. Four shiny plaques on the front doors of the building give more clues of what lies within.

This is Birmingham's Assay Office. It is one of the busiest in the world with up to 100,000 items of jewellery, gems and precious metal passing through here each day to be checked and hallmarked. Birmingham has had its own assay office since 1773 and the hallmark symbol for Birmingham is an anchor. That's an odd choice given Birmingham is one of Britain's cities furthest from the sea but I'll get back to that.

The Brum assay office exists thanks to local big shot and gazillionaire, Matthew Boulton (he's on the back of a fifty pound note, you know). In addition to tinkering with some important stuff for the Industrial Revolution, he was running a silversmith factory. At that time the nearest assay office to Brum was some 70 miles away in Chester. Matt was really miffed about this. The journey to and from Chester risked highway robbery (well before M6 Toll charges) en route and theft of his designs if they got there. So Matt started to lobby parliament to open an assay office in Birmingham and, despite some severe opposition, succeeded. Indeed, he even managed to get agreement for an assay office in Sheffield as they found themselves in a similar situation.

The Birmingham Assay Office opened in 1773 and, naturally, the first customer was Matthew Boulton with some spoons. Probably. Those shiny squares on the front door of the assay

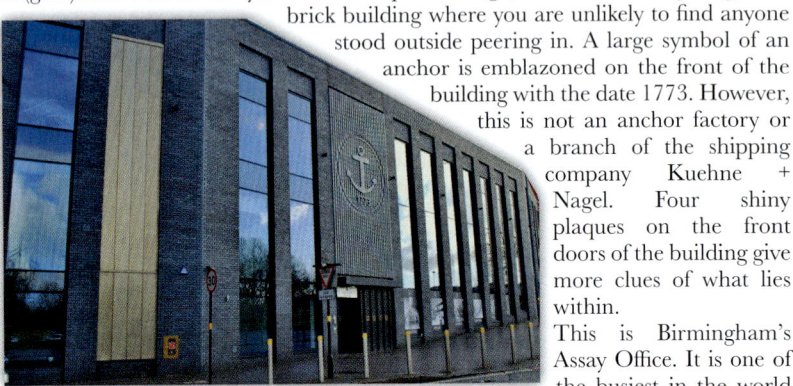

Birmingham Assay Office Shown from Icknield St/ Warstone Lane
///faced.cities.crib

Front Doors of the Assay Office
Hallmark symbols which resemble those first used by the Birmingham Assay Office in 1773.
///faced.cities.crib

58 | The Quirky Guide to Birmingham

office look remarkably like those first hallmarks struck in Birmingham.

Let's get back to that anchor symbol. Birmingham's location doesn't lend itself to strong maritime connections (although the anchor for the Titanic was made in the nearby Black Country) so why an anchor?

The legend goes that Matthew Boulton was staying in a tavern in London called the Crown and Anchor. Upon the toss of a coin it was decided that Sheffield's hallmark symbol would be a crown (subsequently changed to a Yorkshire Rose) and Birmingham's would be an anchor. It's odd to think that the history of Birmingham could have been changed if Boulton had gone for a pint in The Cock and Bull instead.

The Birmingham Assay Office moved to its current location in 2015 after outgrowing its home of almost 140 years on Newhall Street. A number of 'feature' blocks are embedded in the perimeter walls of the new building.

The Previous Assay Office Building
Newhall Street, City Centre
///total.doll.drag

The blocks depict a selection of key hallmark symbols and those used by some of the largest users of the Birmingham Assay Office.

The Mission Statement of the Birmingham Assay Office is 'Protecting the Consumer and Servicing the Trade with Independence and Integrity'. If they feel the urge, they can feel free to add a new tag line the same as this chapter title, 'Keeping in Real, Bab'. No charge.

A Feature Stone on the Assay Office
This one is for Elkington & Co. They made something which is world famous (see page 60)
///unrealistic.firmly.wider

Chapter 25

New Plaques, Please

As children, during the Wimbledon fortnight, it wasn't uncommon to stretch a length of string or a couple of brooms across the back garden or roadside verge and smash a ball to each other using the finest Woolworths rackets.

It turns out that the first time this ever happened was in a Birmingham back garden and that's how tennis was invented. Sort of.

The back garden in question was that of Augurio Perera at his home at 8, Ampton Road Edgbaston. Augurio played the sport of 'racquets' with his Brum born friend Major Thomas Henry ('Harry') Gem. Racquets is similar to the modern game of squash and needed special indoor courts and equipment to play.

Augurio and Harry were irked by the travelling and costs necessary to play racquets so they worked to adapt the game to play outdoors. In the back garden. For free. Sometime between 1859 and 1865 they experimented with a game

8 Ampton Road
Lawn tennis was pioneered in it's back garden
///empty.stud.indeed

that used aspects of racquets and the Basque game of pelota. Their trials pre-date similar games which were being developed around the same time so they are recognised as pioneers of what would become the modern game of tennis.

In the early 1870s Augurio and Harry moved to Leamington Spa and with two local doctors they opened the first lawn tennis club in the world. The rules of the game played there were first published in 1875 and called 'Lawn Tennis or Pelota – Rules of the Game Played by the Leamington Club'. This was the first use of the term 'lawn tennis'. Harry's own, hand annotated, copy of the document is kept in The Library of Birmingham. It is perhaps the only surviving copy of the rules.

Harry Gem's Grave
Warstone Lane Cemetery
///traps.butter.barks

A look at Google Earth revealed that, sadly, there is no tennis court in the back garden of 8 Ampton Road. However, there is one just over the garden fence at 46 Carpenter Road. I propose this is the nearest tennis court in the world to the place where the game originated. New plaque please.

The oldest surviving tennis club in the world is just a tennis ball throw away from Ampton Road. The Edgbaston Archery and Lawn Tennis Society (EALTS) is just over ½ mile away, as the crow flies, on Westbourne Road. The EALTS was founded in 1860 originally as an archery club but tennis was established there by 1875. The current name dates back to 1877 and Harry Gem himself was a once a member.

Edgbaston Archery and Lawn Tennis Society
The modest sign at the entrance to the oldest surviving tennis club in the world.
///entire.unions.lock

The location of EALTS has barely changed over 160 years which means they also have the distinction of being the home of the world's oldest lawn tennis playing surface still in regular use.

Birmingham has another tennis claim to fame. Late in the blazing summer of 1976 at a tennis court at the University of Birmingham, a woman wearing a white tennis dress walks along the court towards the net. She reaches around to her bottom and realises she's had a major wardrobe malfunction. She's forgot to put her pants on. The moment was captured by local photographer Martin Elliott. Martin did a deal with poster retailer Athena and the infamous 'Tennis Girl' poster went on to sell more than 2 million copies. Martin cannily retained the copyright to the photo and some have estimated he earnt royalties of £250,000. Martin died in 2010 aged 63. The woman in the photo never earnt a penny. She is Fiona Butler, who was Martin's girlfriend when the photo was taken.

The homemade dress worn in the photo was sold at auction in 2015 for £15,000 and displayed at the Wimbledon Lawn Tennis Museum. In the same year claims were made by Peter Atkinson that the woman in the photo was not Fiona Butler but his ex wife. Peter offered evidence of similar versions of the photograph which were in circulation prior to 1976. He claimed that Martin photographed his wife in 1972 and it was that photograph which was used for the poster not the later one of Fiona Butler. Nonetheless, Fiona appears to be pretty sure it's her bottom in the photo.

The Site of the Infamous 'Tennis Girl' Photograph
Now student accommodation imaginatively called 'Tennis Courts'. Outdoor games unironically prohibited.
///punk.laying.natively

Sadly, the court where the photo was taken no longer exists. Student accommodation has been built on the site. Maybe it's for the best, lest a steady stream of people show up to recreate the image. I couldn't find any shiny plaques saying 'Fiona Butler showed her bottom on this site in 1976' or similar. A letter to The Birmingham Civic Society me thinks.

The only possible nod to the poster I could find in the area was at other student accommodation. It could just be a coincidence that 'Athena Studios' on Bristol Road has the same name as the company which retailed the poster.

Athena Studios
A homage to the the infamous poster ?
///plans.oasis.scout

If you still need convincing that this heritage doesn't place Birmingham at the centre court of the tennis universe then try one more thing. On that summer weekend when the women and men's singles champions lift their trophies aloft at the Wimbledon finals they are exhibiting Birmingham craftsmanship. Both trophies were made in Brum's Jewellery Quarter by Elkington & Co in the 19th century.

Chapter 26

The Last House in Birmingham

For many years The Guinness Book of Records listed 2679 Stratford Road, B94 5NH as the highest numbered house in Britain. It still is, as far as I can tell. I thought that's a nice, easy, quite interesting fact to include in the book. Birmingham has the highest numbered house in the country. Tick.

But my usual, relentless fact checking (sniggers) uncovered a problem. I had thought that because the house had a Birmingham postcode it must be in Birmingham, right? No.

It turns out the Birmingham 'B' postcode is the largest in the country. It covers a larger population (1.9 million) and more postcode districts (77) than any other in the UK. That means the Birmingham post code is far reaching. Like, really far reaching – well beyond the confines of the 10 constituencies (see page 5) and 69 wards which make up the current metropolitan district of the City of Birmingham.

This got me wondering, where is the last house in Birmingham? After some thorough research on Google Earth I reckon it's Fox Cottage, Bickmarsh, Bidford-on-Avon. At least it is as far as 'B' post codes are concerned, but I'm pretty sure the good people of Bickmarsh wouldn't consider themselves Brummies. It's around 24 miles as the crow flies from Fox Cottage to Victoria Square in Brum. That makes the cottage closer to the centre of Cheltenham than Birmingham.

So, where is the real last house in Birmingham? A house that falls within the confines of the City of Birmingham (put crudely, Birmingham City Council collect your bins). Well, after more time on Google Earth I think it's a house on Camp Road, Sutton Coldfield which is 9.4 miles, as the crow flies, from Victoria Square. I declare this the location of the last house in Birmingham – there is no residential property farther from the centre than this.

But let's get back to where we started and that highest house number in Britain. Firstly, it could have been a much higher number. Stratford Road starts in Sparkbrook near Birmingham City Centre and ten miles will be clocked up before you reach that highest house number on the same road.

The Highest Numbered House in Britain
Birmingham post code but definitely not in Birmingham.
Stratford Road, Hockley Heath.
///sundial.foiled.guitar

The Last House in Birmingham
More than 9 miles from the City Centre.
Camp Road, Sutton Coldfield

62 | The Quirky Guide to Birmingham

However, at one point where house numbers have already reached well into the 1600s they give up and start again from number 1. The odd and even numbers also swap to the opposite sides of the road. This leads to the rather incongruous situation of 1659 Stratford Road being next door neighbour to no. 2 Stratford Road. So why? Did someone lose count? Or run out of numbers? Well, no. It all seems to be because of boundaries. The numbering re-starts where Stratford Road crosses the boundary from Birmingham to Solihull. And as many residents of Solihull (Silhillians) will tell you, Solihull is emphatically not part of Birmingham.

Consequently, the highest house number in Britain is not in Birmingham but in Solihull. As if that weren't enough, by the same quirk of boundaries, Birmingham Airport is also not actually in Birmingham.

As this book is all about Birmingham I shouldn't even have brought it up. Sorry.

The Incongruous House Numbering of Stratford Road
Number 2 is next door to 1659
///puff.price.minus

Solihull Boundary
It's not Birmingham but is home to the highest house number in Britain. And Birmingham Airport.
///frozen.dating.banks

Chapter 27

We Was Robbed

Aston Villa is one of the oldest football clubs in the world and a founding member of the English Football League. Villa have had their ups and downs over the years but they do have seven FA Cup wins and the European Cup on their list of achievements.

However, there is at least one aspect in which the club is unrivalled and unbeaten. All-time record holders for losing trophies. I don't mean losing matches that lead to trophies, I mean losing the actual trophies once they've got their hands on them.

Villa's second FA Cup win was in 1895. It was a local derby between West Bromwich Albion and Aston Villa which Villa won 1-0 (which, incidentally, included the fastest goal ever scored in FA Cup final history until 2009). Villa were awarded the trophy and, in those days, the winning team retained the cup in their possession until the next final. The original FA Cup trophy was called 'The Little Tin Idol' and was much smaller and different in design to the one we are familiar with today. Birmingham businessman William Shillcock was a renowned sporting goods manufacturer and had a shop on New Town Row. After Villa's success Shillcock asked Villa if he could display the trophy in his shop window and they agreed. Prior to display the trophy was insured for today's equivalent of £20,000 – much more than the original purchase cost of £2000 equivalent. This was to prove a very prudent move; sometime on the evening of 11th September, the trophy was stolen from the shop.

Shillcock was apparently distraught by the loss and offered to pay a substantial reward for its return. As time marched on there was no sign of the trophy and a replacement was needed in time for the next FA Cup final. As luck would have it, one of Villa's ex-players was Howard Vaughton whose grandfather was the founder of Vaughtons, a local silversmith. Vaughtons produced an exact replica of the original trophy which was paid for using the £3000 equivalent fine that had been imposed upon Villa for losing the original. The replica continued to be used until 1910 when it was replaced with the trophy design we are familiar with today. The replica 'Little Tin Idol' was sold at auction in 2005 for £478,000 to the then Chairman of Birmingham City FC, David Gold. It is currently safely on display at the National Football Museum in Manchester.

The original trophy has never been recovered. Decades later a local career criminal claimed

The Original Vaughton Works
With another inaccurate shiny plaque. They did not make the original FA Cup but a replica when the original was stolen.
Livery Street
///serves.drip.hello

Shillcock Grove
A nod to the owner of the shop from where the original FA Cup was stolen
///rinse.pets.hugs

64 | The Quirky Guide to Birmingham

responsibility for the theft and that the trophy had been melted down although doubt was poured upon his story.

Vaughtons are still manufacturing in Birmingham and continue to make the FA Cup winners medals. Shillcock's shop is long gone and it would have been no comfort to him whatsoever that a nearby street took his name years after his death.

Fast forward 87 years from the FA cup theft to 26th May 1982. Villa are in Rotterdam about to play Bayern Munich in the final of the European Cup. What happened is immortalised in the television commentary of Brian Moore which adorns a banner across the North Stand of Villa Park: 'Shaw, Williams, prepared to venture down the left. There's a good ball in for Tony Morley. Oh, it must be and it is! It's Peter Withe'. Withe scored the only goal of the match. Villa had won the European cup for the first and only time (so far) and the sixth time in succession for an English club.

What followed was the well-used script for 'we've just won a major football title'. The trophy is pictured on players' heads, in the cockpit of the plane flying home and on the plane steps when it lands back in Blighty. Pull the dust sheets off the open top bus for a parade through the City Centre, a civic reception at the council house and waving the trophy from the balcony to thousands of fans and well-wishers assembled in Victoria Square below. A star on Broad Street follows decades later and fans still experience a warm, fuzzy, nostalgic feeling when they think back to Villa's night of European glory.

Villa's Place on the Walk of Stars
Placed 27 years after their win.
Broad Street
///title.sleeps.rests

But there were nearly very different, embarrassing headlines and a twist to the story that for almost thirty years very few people knew about.

In 2010 West Bar Police Station in Sheffield was being emptied for closure and some curious photographs were unearthed. The photographs showed various police officers at the station with what looked like the European Cup trophy. So it was that the unlikely journey of the trophy then became public.

The Villa team and trophy had been back in Brum only a matter of hours before two players, Colin Gibson and Gordon Cowans, decided to take the trophy to the pub. As you do. The Fox in Hopwas was a known Villa player haunt at the time and the players thought it would be nice for some fans to see the trophy and get photos with it. The players got involved in a serious darts match and at one heart stopping moment realised the trophy, about the size and weight of a large traffic cone, was gone. Complete with the claret and blue ribbons still attached.

The Fox, Hopwas
The European Cup trophy was 'borrowed' from here in 1982
///processor.shower.afflicted

Shortly afterwards the culprit was showing off the trophy to friends 100 miles away but eventually relented and handed the trophy in to the police station giving a false name. It was too good an opportunity for the dazed police to pass up. A hastily arranged football match ensued at the station to play for the European Cup. The scenes (including the obligatory trophy on a police officer's head) would be captured for posterity using the crime scene camera. West Midlands police retrieved the cup from their South Yorkshire colleagues in plenty of time for the trophy's outing on the open top bus.

Most people were none the wiser but may have been intrigued by the dents the trophy seemed to have picked up along the way.

Chapter 28

Flag

Birmingham didn't have a flag which could be freely flown by the public (a 'community flag') until 2015. Until then the only flag representing the city was a banner of arms (based upon the Birmingham coat of arms) which can only be flown by the City Council.

The new flag design was chosen through a competition. The winning design from 470 entries was from 10 year olds Thomas Keogh and David Smith.

The flag colours and zig zag style is reminiscent of some features of the original flag but there is more hidden meaning to the design. The blue triangles form an abstract letter 'B' for Birmingham and are blue as a representation of the City's canals. The golden zig-zag represents closed lock gates on the blue canals but also a letter 'M' on its side. M is the Roman letter for 1000 and recalls 'the City of a thousand trades'. Lastly, the central bulls head recalls the Bull Ring.

Many Brummies don't yet recognise the flag and it is yet to be flown widely in the City.

Chapter 29
Battle Royal

There are just eight places in Britain which can use the 'Royal' title. Only one can call itself 'The Royal Town'; The Royal Town of Sutton Coldfield. And yes, unlike Solihull (see page 62), it is part of Birmingham. And therein lies a tale or two.

Sutton Coldfield (I'm going to omit 'The Royal Town of' from now on just for ease of reading and my laziness in typing) is the largest of Birmingham's 10 constituencies but has by far the lowest population density. Almost a fifth of the constituency area is covered by leafy Sutton Park, one of the largest urban parks in Europe. Sutton Coldfield is the most affluent Brum constituency and is home to the second most expensive street in Birmingham (Hartopp Road) where the average house price is £1.3m. It's the sort of place where you can bump into the local MP[1] or a footballer's celebrity partner[2] at the local Waitrose (before it closed down). The sort of place where you could imagine Peter and Jane[3] from the Ladybird Books living the suburban dream. You get the picture.

But all is not peaceful in suburbia. For fifty years battles have been cordially raging. A clue to the cause of this unrest, if one was needed, can be found on the satirical map of the various quarters of Birmingham published by Paradise Circus in 2013. Sutton Coldfield is shown as the 'Doesn't Want To Be In Birmingham Quarter'.

For centuries Sutton Coldfield was largely in charge of its own destiny and looked after its own affairs. The legend goes that King Henry VIII was out hunting in the area with his local buddy, Bishop Vesey. The King was confronted by a wild boar but was saved from being savaged when a young girl stepped in and shot the animal with a silver arrow. The King expressed his gratitude by granting Sutton Coldfield a charter for its freedom.

The legend may be spurious, but the facts are clear. Henry VIII signed the Royal Charter for Sutton Coldfield in 1528 and in his own written words he decreed, "And that the same town and village shall for ever hereafter be accounted, named, and called, The Royal Town of Sutton Coldfield, in our County of Warwick." King Charles II

*Apropos Arrows
Just inside this archway on the left-hand wall you can see a number of vertical grooves which have been worn into the stone blocks. They are said to be from when archers sharpened their arrowheads hundreds of years ago, maybe before practising or hunting in Sutton Park.
5, Coleshill Street
///fetch.cans.belts

---

1   Since 2001, *The Right Honourable Andrew Mitchell MP (Conservative)*
2   *Helen Flanagan, best known for playing Rosie Webster in Coronation Street. Her fiancé is Scott Sinclair who played football for local teams Birmingham City, West Bromwich Albion and Aston Villa before moving on in 2016.*
3   *Actually, they did. Almost. Harry Wingfield was one of the main artists for the Ladybird 'Peter and Jane' books (official name 'The Ladybird Key Words Reading Scheme'). He lived a stone's throw beyond the Sutton Coldfield border in Little Aston and employed local children as models/ inspiration for his illustrations.*

also signed a Royal Charter for Sutton Coldfield in 1676, confirming the rights and benefits granted by Henry VIII.

Part of King Henry's gift was also Sutton Park. The Charter laid down that the inhabitants might 'freely hunt fish and fowl there, with dogs, bows and arrows, and with other engines for deer, stags, hares, foxes and other wild beasts.' There's not much hunting of wild beasts going on these days but Sutton Park is still a largely unspoilt area enjoyed by the public.

The charter determined that the town would be governed by a Warden and Society. King Henry's Tudor Rose proliferated all over the town and, much later, mock Tudor wooden signs at the town limits ensured you knew that you were entering 'The Royal Town of Sutton Coldfield'.

It wasn't until 1885 that Sutton Coldfield saw the next major change to its governance. It was still independent but became a municipal borough led by a mayor, aldermen and councillors.

Then, the bombshell. In the early 1970s an intended national reform of local government was announced and the intention that Sutton Coldfield would cease to be a borough and instead become part of, gulp, Birmingham.

Many Suttonians were not happy. Apoplectic more like. 'Save Sutton' stickers started to appear, hundreds protested on Downing Street, hundreds more wrote to the Prime Minister (Edward Heath). Mocked up pictures appeared of flats built in Sutton Park. A Whittock cartoon appeared in the press showing an enraged man at home in Sutton Coldfield resorting to alcohol with a caption '…to top the day someone called him a Brummie'.

But the protests went unheeded. On April Fool Day 1974 Sutton Coldfield became part of the Metropolitan Borough of Birmingham and ended the unbroken chain of wardens and mayors of the Royal Town since 1528.

Changes started to be seen but Suttonians didn't always take them lying down.

Brummies, and anyone else for that matter, could now enter Sutton Park for free, a privilege which was only previously extended to Suttonians. Eventually, even Suttonians would actually have to pay, like everyone else, to enter the park. By car. At weekends. In the summer.

The green street name signs which had distinguished Sutton Coldfield began to be substituted with the black and white ones of Birmingham. There were many

The Ubiquitous Rose of The Royal Town
A small selection from around the historic Town Centre.

///audio.bring.rush
///fits.mugs.badly
///audio.bring.rush
///pocket.rings.guards
///jolly.chats.volunteered
///coast.cri.dark

The Yo-yo Royal Signs
Up, down and now up again. This is an original example from the 1930s saved from destruction by a previous Mayoress of the Town.
///shapes.patch.calculating

The Quirky Guide to Birmingham | 69

examples of the new signs being defaced or vandalised with a common target being the Birmingham Coat of Arms. In at least one case the new sign contained a spelling mistake. Even as late as 2012, a spate of new stickers started to be applied to the street signs to obliterate the Birmingham coat of arms. Many stickers still remain.

The original wooden 'Royal' sign now cut a forlorn figure behind new signs on the border proclaiming 'County of West Midlands' and 'City of Birmingham'. These signs too were the target of vandalism.

Sutton Coldfield did win some of the battles though. The Birmingham Coat of Arms was updated to include some specific representation of Sutton Coldfield. The Tudor Rose was added as was a Bishop's Mitre, representative of Bishop Vesey whose coat of arms was the basis of the Sutton Coldfield arms.

Of all the changes though, perhaps the worst was that after more than 400 years Sutton Coldfield would lose its 'Royal' status when it merged with Birmingham.

Signs of the Times
Top: A street sign which was defaced to cover the Birmingham Coat of Arms ///acid.swift.actors
Middle left: A close up of the sticker covering the coat of arms from above
Middle right: A rare pre 1974 survivor of when Sutton Coldfield was a borough. ///vine.office.racks
Bottom: Another rare survivor; a green street sign pre-dating the agglomeration with Birmingham. ///afford.staple.ladder

Coats of Arms
How the Coat of Arms of Birmingham was modified to adopt elements from the Sutton Coldfield Coat of Arms

Sutton Coldfield Coat of Arms
At Vesey Gardens, Sutton Coldfield.
///front.lions.highs

Birmingham Coat of Arms
On almost every street name sign

The last Mayor and Mayoress of Sutton Coldfield (Donald and Julia Mills) had picked up the mantle to retain the Royal moniker. They wrote a letter to the Queen urging her to support a petition to retain the Royal connection and delivered it personally to Buckingham Palace when they attended a garden party there. As you do. They even suggested a compromise of substituting the term 'Royal' for 'Regis' to maintain the connection. The reply that came later from the Home Office must have been something of a shock. The Royal title had already been lost more than a hundred years earlier. The Home Office argued that when Sutton Coldfield became a borough in 1885 the Royal status was lost and Sutton Coldfield had never been a Royal Borough.

Further protests ensued but to no avail. This battle was lost. Sutton Coldfield was Royal no more and those nice, mock Tudor 'Royal' signs at the borders eventually started to disappear. But Suttonians don't give up easily. Fast forward 40 years and there was new impetus behind a campaign to restore the Royal connection. The local MP, newspaper (Sutton Coldfield Observer), Sutton Coldfield Civic Society and various residents joined forces to bring back Royal. In 2014 they received the confirmation they wanted; that Sutton Coldfield was free to use the Royal description again. In fact, they never lost it. Phew.

The wooden 'Royal' signs could be erected once again. Yay. There were some new ones but at least one original which the last Mayoress (Julia Mills) of the town had had the foresight to save from destruction some years earlier. The next battle was to convince the map producers to show the full Royal name on their maps. It took a further four years but ultimately Google did relent in 2018 and you can now see The Royal Town of Sutton Coldfield in its full glory on their maps.

After 1974 Donald and Julia Mills, and many others, continued to campaign for independence from Birmingham. In 2015, their determination yielded fruit. An official ballot of locals was undertaken asking whether they wanted an independent Town Council to be established. 70% of the votes were in favour. In 2016 The Royal Sutton Coldfield Town Council was established. The old robes, chains of office and mace were taken out of a museum for once again Sutton Coldfield had a mayor of its own and a degree of autonomy for the first time in forty years.

Back to 2020 and the battles still aren't over. Just like 500 years ago the hunting ground is Sutton Park. The latest strategic plan of the Town Council includes an objective that the management and ownership of Sutton Park should rest with the Town Council and not Birmingham City Council. Let's just say that, so far, not everyone is entirely aligned with the objective.

Vesey Gardens
Named after Bishop Vesey. A golden statue of him and the Sutton Coldfield coat of arms can be seen in the distance.
///front.lions.highs

Chapter 30

The Final Victim

When I started writing this book most people had never heard of 'R' values. Terms like 'lockdown' and 'shielding' were only normally encountered in Hollywood blockbusters and quarantine was just for animals. Then, along came Covid-19 and we all quickly became more acquainted with the language of virology. During one early news item about Covid-19 the expert interviewee made an intriguing reference to a past requirement for quarantine in Birmingham. I had no idea what he was talking about so, naturally, I investigated. What I discovered was the tragic, and still mysterious, story of the last ever recorded person in the world to die of smallpox.

Thankfully, smallpox is seldom a point of conversation these days. Probably because the United Nations declared in 1980 that the disease had been eradicated from the earth. But the last recorded death from the disease was just two years earlier and not in some far away land. It happened right here in Birmingham to local woman Janet Parker and her death would have enduring consequences for the virus worldwide.

University of Birmingham Medical School
The East Wing of the school where there was once a smallpox laboratory on the ground floor and Janet Parker worked as a photographer on the floor above.
Vincent Drive
///vines.froth.normal

Whilst Covid-19 has caused death and misery worldwide it is nothing compared to Smallpox. If you've ever seen photos of smallpox victims you're unlikely to forget them. It is a truly terrible, ancient disease that has killed hundreds of millions of people over the centuries and left countless others blinded and disfigured. Humanity declared a war upon the disease and eventually a vaccination was found and deployed globally. Even in the late 1960s millions globally were still affected by the disease and vaccination continued to be common in the UK despite the rarity of the disease here.

One of those vaccinated against smallpox in the 1960s was Janet Parker. In 1978 Janet was 40, a professional photographer living with her husband in Kings Heath. She was working at the University of Birmingham Medical School in the anatomy department. In the same building Professor Henry Bedson, a virologist, was conducting research into smallpox. His laboratory was on the floor below Janet's workplace. In August 1978 they were both about to have their worlds turned upside down.

Britain used to have many isolation hospitals, especially established to treat patients with highly contagious diseases such as tuberculosis, diphtheria and smallpox. The low incidence of these diseases by the 1970s meant that there was just one hospital left in the UK; the National Isolation Hospital at Catherine De Barnes in Solihull. For most of the time this hospital didn't have any patients but it had to be ready to receive them with just one hour's notice. On the afternoon of 20th August 1978 the hospital received the call that it never wanted and a seemingly very efficient government machine kicked into action. Later that evening Janet Parker was on a ward at Catherine de Barnes and before the day was out her parents and other close contacts were in quarantine. A little more than a week later 500 people were in quarantine. No stone was left unturned to find people who may have had contact with Janet. A young girl guide who had sold her ice skates to Janet was tracked down on a camping trip. Even the three £1 notes payment the girl received were confiscated for risk of contamination.

A little more than three weeks after her admission, Janet died at Catherine De Barnes. She was the only fatality of smallpox in this outbreak but alas not the only death connected with the incident. Sadly, Janet's father, Frederick Witcomb, died of a cardiac arrest aged 71 whilst in quarantine at Catherine de Barnes. If the authority machinery was being efficient to contain the disease the media machine was being equally efficient in its haste to allocate blame and the easy choice was Professor Bedson. The day after Frederick's death, Professor Bedson went to his garden shed, cut his own throat and died a few days later aged 48. His suicide note read 'I am sorry to have misplaced the trust which so many of my friends and colleagues have placed in me and my work.'

The investigation into the outbreak concluded that Janet Parker caught smallpox at the Medical School most likely via transmission through ventilation ducts which pass from floor to floor in the building. This conclusion was later placed into significant doubt during a court case which some consider also exonerated Professor Bedson. To this day it remains a mystery exactly how Janet Parker contracted smallpox.

Following the incident all known stocks of smallpox worldwide were ordered to be destroyed or sent for storage in just two laboratories in the USA and Russia. They remain the only two places approved by the World Health Organisation to retain smallpox.

There had been an earlier outbreak of smallpox in Birmingham in 1966 and it is likely that during that time Janet Parker received the smallpox vaccine as a precaution. There were no deaths during the 1966 outbreak and the reported primary case was Tony McLennan. In a curious twist, like Janet, he too was a photographer at the University of Birmingham Medical School.

Catherines Close, Solihull
Previous site of the National Isolation Hospital and where the last victim of smallpox died. Now desirable homes.
///badge.record.plants

Postscript – The Catherine De Barnes Isolation Hospital. When one of Birmingham's Isolation Hospitals (Witton) outlived its use in the 1960s it was deliberately burnt down by the authorities with the intention of destroying any remaining traces of disease. When the Isolation Hospital at Catherine De Barnes was similarly defunct in the 1980s you could be excused for thinking it met a similar end. But no. Instead the buildings were fumigated and developed into prime residential properties. A comparison of the site today to the 1940s shows a remarkably similar layout of the buildings. This leads me to the macabre possibility that in someone's pleasant Catherines Close home there perhaps once stood the ward bed of Janet Parker, the last recorded person in the world to die from smallpox.

Chapter 31
Walked All Over

Even near some of Birmingham's most recognised sights and busiest streets you can find some surprises which thousands of people have literally walked over without a second glance or knowing what history lies beneath their feet. This chapter highlights a few favourites.

At the foot of the statue of Queen Victoria in Victoria Square you will find one of the paving stones engraved 'Ebony' and a paw print. It has little to do with Queen Victoria herself.

In the early 1990s Victoria Square was undergoing major refurbishment. One of the workers was local stonemason Larry Dae. He was often accompanied by his Black Labrador, Ebony, resplendent in her own high-vis vest and helping carry tools. Ebony's contribution is marked with the plaque.

///cities.tent.pound

Not far away from Ebony, you can find these glass light wells in the pavement behind the Council House on Edmund Street. If you're brave enough to kneel down and peer through one of the cracks in the glass you'll notice the walls and ceilings of the rooms below are fully tiled in old fashioned cream coloured ceramic tiles. It could be mistaken for underground public conveniences but the truth is altogether more macabre. You are looking into history of when these subterranean rooms were used as a morgue. During World War II fatalities from bombings or fires would be stored here if hospital mortuary space was full.

///gone.trails.fleet

As you walk around the city centre you may frequently come across metal studs in the pavement engraved 'BCC'. BCC stands for Birmingham City Council and the studs are property boundary markers (not to be mistaken for grids of metal studs which sometimes appear near road crossings for the benefit of the visually impaired).

The boundary of a property may go beyond the obvious building. The boundary could protrude into the pavement/ road or the roof may overhang the walls. The studs mark where there may be a change in the rules or law that applies to the land/ property, such as how far to go setting up tables/ chairs on the pavement.

74 | The Quirky Guide to Birmingham

START/ FINISH

Superprix
The route of the 2.5 mile race circuit on Brum's streets.

Contra Flow
Unusually the race was run in a counter clockwise direction and against the normal flow of traffic. Allegedly, this was to discourage Brummies from doing their best Nigel Mansell impersonation and racing around the circuit themselves. It also meant that some of the protective barriers had been erected incorrectly and had to be hastily re-erected to ensure they provided the correct protection to match the direction of travel.

Bromsgrove Street
Pershore Street
Bristol Street
Sherlock Street
Belgrave Middleway

This book exalts many mundane items, but I award top prize for mundanity to this one. Yes, you are looking at a screw in an access cover in the ground. How on Earth could this have any significance? But this screw does have a connection to Birmingham's history. Despite occasional spates of theft, manhole covers and the like are not normally screwed down. Their weight is generally sufficient to keep them in place. So what was the imperative to particularly keep this cover, and many others like it, from going astray?

There was a time when Birmingham aspired to be the new Monaco and hold a Formula 1 race on the streets of Brum (a long time before Singapore had its chance).

As a precursor to a topflight race, the Birmingham Superprix was born and from 1986 until 1990 Formula 3 street races were held. There were many festivities with things like a man flying about strapped to a rocket pack. The first Superprix was held over August bank holiday weekend so, naturally, it lashed down with rain and lots of cars crashed prior to the race being 'red-flagged'.

Metal covers along the entire 2.5 mile circuit were screwed down by the utility companies. The reason? It was feared that the speed and grip of the racing tyres could suck the covers from their housings and launch them skywards. Which apparently isn't good for safety when driving at 180mph.

Racing Line
There are still some more noticeable remnants of the racing circuit. This island (roundabout) at Haden Circus still has a strange layout in the centre due to the race.
///same.covers.clubs

The Quirky Guide to Birmingham | 75

In another example of 'just because it's got a shiny plaque doesn't mean it's true' (see page 22), a plaque in the pavement on Newhall Hill shows a depiction of the current FA Cup design and states 'the FA Cup was designed here'. The plaque forms part of the 'Charm Bracelet Trail' (see page 86) but it isn't correct. It is true that the current design of the FA Cup trophy was made by the company Fattorini & Sons in 1911 and a little further along from the plaque on Newhall Hill is indeed a branch of Fattorini in the jewellery quarter. The trouble is, it wasn't the Birmingham branch of Fattorini that was responsible for the FA Cup. Fattorini's own website says it was designed in their Bradford office. Now, it might just be that the plaque refers obtusely to an earlier version of the FA cup, but that's a different story (which you can find on page 64). And still wasn't designed in Birmingham.
///aspect.repair.reward

For more than 200 years the measurement of a 'metre' was based upon the length of a metal rod kept in France. It's pretty basic but at least everyone could relate to it. Then, in 1960, some bright sparks decided that a metre could be determined by the wavelengths of the emissions of a krypton atom and later it was determined by the speed of light. Which nobody could relate to other than those with a PhD in physics. Anyway, as Master of the House Monsieur Thénardier so eloquently sang in Les Misérables 'Watering the wine, making up the weight, Pickin' up their knick-knacks when they can't see straight', there is always someone who wants to sell you short. Whether it's the butcher with his proverbial thumb on the scales or the publican serving a skant pint. These days it's relatively easy to check if someone has diddled you. All manner of trustworthy measuring devices are readily available, but it hasn't always been so. In bygone times these brass plaques set into Victoria Square allowed the public to check if they really had been sold a true foot, metre, pole or link. Whatever that is. Similar public standards of length can also be found in Trafalgar Square (London) and the Royal Observatory, Greenwich.
///chose.twist.woke

76 | The Quirky Guide to Birmingham

If you're wondering how a huge meteorite landing in the city centre managed to escape your attention, it didn't. In 2000 the Ikon Gallery commissioned conceptual artist Cornelia Parker to create a pyrotechnics display from the top of the Rotunda. The fireworks contained powdered fragments from the meteorite thus generating a meteorite shower over the Bullring as well as a fabulous display. The Ikon described the firework display in a way only the artworld can: 'it signaled (sic) a strong commitment to presenting the best contemporary art outside dedicated 'art space', asserting a refreshing freedom in artistic practice and the possibility of an apprehension of beauty anywhere'. Okie dokey.

///media.double.note

Chapter 32

The Long and Short of it

The tallest person ever recorded in England was a Brummie. During her lifetime she was possibly the tallest living person on the planet and for decades was recorded as the tallest woman that ever lived. She died young without ever knowing the records she had set and desecration awaited her in death. No photographs, if they exist, have ever emerged publicly of this 'Northfield giantess'.

Jane 'Ginny' Bunford was born in Bartley Green in 1895. Aged around 11 she received a head injury which seemed to trigger her excessive growth. If they were marking her height on the door frame they would have run out of space when Jane was 13. She was 6'6". She kept growing but developed curvature of the spine which prevented her from standing up straight. Her height, adjusted for the curvature, peaked at 7'11". She took a size 17 shoe. The length from the end of her wrist to the tip of her middle finger was a little more than the span of this open book. Descriptions of Jane are striking. She spoke with a deep voice but had a gentle nature. Her copper coloured hair also made it into the record books as being in excess 8 feet long. It would often be tied into thick plaits but when loose it was as if she was wearing a cloak.

Sadly, giants often do not lead long lives. Jane's childhood bang on the head would ultimately lead to her demise. She died in 1922 from hyperpituitarism and gigantism aged just 26. She was buried in the original churchyard of St Michaels and All Angels Church, Bartley Green on 5th April 1922. It didn't take long for rumours to start that there was something not quite right about Jane's funeral.

Things came to a head 50 years later with rather macabre revelations. It started when the Guinness Book of Records got wind of a skeleton of a giant being kept by the Anatomical Museum in the Medical School of Birmingham University (now University of Birmingham). A photograph of the skeleton was included in the 1971 edition of the Guinness Book of Records and described as 'the tallest woman of all time'. The identity of the giant was not revealed, just that it was a fifty-year-old secret. The book did

Memorial to a Giant of Birmingham
Installed at Bartley Green Library in 2000. In 2013 a short cul-de-sac nearby, Bunford Close, was named after Jane.

Adams Hill, Bartley Green
///client.hours.skinny

These two silhouettes show the comparative heights of Jane Bunford and Nanette Stocker

78 | The Quirky Guide to Birmingham

divulge that the woman died in Northfield in 1922. Given that Northfield isn't a mythical land of giants, it didn't take Columbo to deduce that the skeleton could be Jane.

The story was picked up in early 1972 by local television, ATV. Their investigation mooted the possibility that the university skeleton was Jane. This shocked some of Jane's relatives, one of whom alleged a case of body snatching. The University initially remained tight lipped but eventually conceded that the skeleton was indeed Jane Bunford.

In the 1972 edition of the Guinness Book of Records they published Jane's name and details for the first time as the 'World, All-time Tallest Giantess'. On the book's front cover they included an illustration of Jane's skeleton on display in a fictitious shop window.

It has never been divulged how Jane's skeleton came into the possession of the university. Some accounts suggested that Jane's father gave permission for the body to go to medical science. Difficult, considering he died years before Jane did.

What Lies Beneath?
When interviewed in 1972, this is the site that the gravedigger pointed out as the 1922 grave of Jane Bunford. There was no marker in '72 and still isn't.
Field Lane, Bartley Green
///lung.cope.bleak

It took more than 30 years and a law change for the skeleton to be returned to Jane's relatives in 2005 and be buried in a private ceremony in an unmarked grave.

What happened to Jane's body has been the subject of much hearsay and conjecture. The local rumour was that pall bearers reported the coffin was too light and Jane couldn't have been in there. The coffin was apparently locked in the church the night before the funeral. The first time it had ever happened to the recollection of the gravedigger. The gruesome speculation of one of Jane's cousins was that Jane's skeleton was removed from her body prior to burial and only what remained was buried.

Without an exhumation it will remain a mystery of who or what lies in Jane's original grave.

Nannette Stocker (aka Nanetta, Manetta) was much the opposite of Jane Bunford. She stood just 2'9" tall which earnt her the label of 'the smallest woman ever in this Kingdom'. Born in Austria, Nannette was quite a large baby and grew quickly until aged four but then grew no more She garnered attention to her diminutive stature by making a living in show business. She toured Europe and later teamed up with John Hauptmann who was just three inches taller than Nannette and was liberated from a French institution. They would draw large crowds with their performances; dancing, playing the piano and violin. Nannette was due to appear in Birmingham in 1819 but died aged 39 whilst staying in the city. She was buried in St Philip's Cathedral churchyard where her grave can still be seen. Nannette's resting place is in comparatively good condition thanks to renovation in 1935 but the headstone originally stood 33 inches high, the same as Nanette, but has since shrunk in stature.

///drive.string.eggs

The Quirky Guide to Birmingham | 79

Chapter 33

What a Relief

One of the largest pieces of art in Birmingham would amply cover half a tennis court but you can be forgiven if it has escaped your attention. Most of the Grade II listed artwork has been covered up, literally for the sake of fashion. The 'Rotunda Relief' was installed in the 1960s when the Rotunda was constructed. It was originally the centrepiece of the main banking hall of Lloyds Bank, a space which is now taken by the Zara store. The huge, abstract mural made from a type of concrete was created by renowned local sculptor A. John Poole. Like the Rotunda, the full artwork is completely circular and is two stories high but is only partially visible on the first floor of Zara.

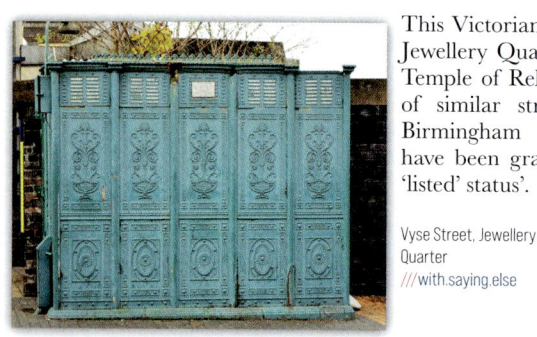

This Victorian era cast iron urinal in the Jewellery Quarter has been named 'The Temple of Relief'. It is one of a number of similar structures in Birmingham which have been granted 'listed' status'.

Vyse Street, Jewellery Quarter
///with.saying.else

'The Temple of Relief'
Grade 2 Listed Cast Iron Urinal manufactured circa 1880 at the Walter Macfarlane Saracen Foundry, Scotland
Designed with a 'Floral Adamish' Pattern one of three distinct types used

Health and Safety in the 1960s wasn't quite the same as today. Hence, the concept of constructing a climbing wall, with nice, sharp, hard concrete and an equally hard landing was the natural thing to entertain the kids back then. We'll put it at a major road junction too so that the air quality's good.
These Brutalist, abstract murals were designed by sculptor William Mitchell and installed in 1968. They really were designed for climbing, but I really wouldn't recommend it.
More slightly scary places under major roads can be found on page 24.

Beneath Hockley Circus
///doors.exile.tooth

80 | The Quirky Guide to Birmingham

///slate.copies.assume

OLD SQUARE

Lloyds Bank was founded in Birmingham in 1765 by Sampson Lloyd II and John Taylor (yes, the same John Taylor as on page 38). Sampson's son, Sampson Lloyd III or 'Sampy', was also a co-founder of the bank. Sampy lived at no.13 Old Square when it was a very grand square of Georgian abodes for the great and the good of Birmingham. In his thirties, Sampy married 16 year old Rachael Barnes. They got real busy and had 17 children together. One of their 10 daughters, also called Rachael (you can understand how they may have run out of ideas for names), married William Summerfield. Sadly, Rachael died whilst giving birth to their only child, a son, who survived. William soon found consolation with his wife's sister Anne (Nancy) Lloyd. They consoled each other's brains out, you might say. It was more than eighteenth century Quaker family values could take and Nancy and William eloped to Gretna Green to be married and eventually had eight children of their own. That's all very interesting you might think (I hope) but what's it got to do with this mural.

This mural, also called 'Old Square', is a fibreglass artwork created in 1967 by Kenneth Budd (see page 34 for another of his works) and originally located in a below street level shopping precinct. The relief depicts various aspects of the history of Old Square and if you look closely you'll see young Nancy climbing down a ladder to run off with William. The mural also shows a beehive which was the original symbol of Lloyd's Bank before black horses ran amok. You can still see beehives on buildings which were, or still are, branches of Lloyd's, like this one (right) on the High Street, Sutton Coldfield.

///silks.rarely.poet

Chapter 34

You Can See My House From Here

At the edges of the Birmingham conurbation you can quickly find yourself in open countryside and winding roads. A lay-by on one such winding road affords a great panoramic view of Birmingham (weather permitting).

Whilst you take in the view and try to spot your abode (good luck, I recommend binoculars) you won't be able to miss the two large lakes in the foreground. They aren't really lakes but man-made reservoirs which contain water that has been on a long journey. Virtually every home, factory, hospital, office block, hotel and university you can see from here all have one thing in common. They all drink and consume water sourced from those two reservoirs.

Most of the water in the reservoirs originated from the Elan Valley in mid-Wales. It takes around two days for the water to make the 73 mile journey through pipelines and tunnels (aqueduct) until it sees the light of day again in those reservoirs. The route of the aqueduct used to be shown on some public maps, but this ended following a bomb attack on the pipeline in 1968 which caused significant disruption.

BT Tower

Alpha Tower

Caban Coch Dam in Elan Valley, Mid Wales
The origin of the water before its 73 mile journey to Birmingham
///safety.ruling.topic

82 | The Quirky Guide to Birmingham

Perhaps the most amazing thing about the water's long voyage is that it uses only gravity. It never sees a pump during the whole journey. Just think about that for a minute. Imagine setting off on a 73 mile bike ride from Wales to Birmingham which goes uphill and down but you never have to pedal once the whole trip. That's sort of what the mutton chopped, tall hatted (I imagine) engineers that designed the super-efficient aqueduct achieved more than a 120 years ago without so much as a laptop in sight.

For generations this triumph of Victorian engineering has been vital for Birmingham's water supply. There have been changes and improvements over the years and the current owners, Severn Trent Water, have recently been spending more than £300 million to improve the resilience of Birmingham's water supply.

But still, the aqueduct goes on silently and reliably bringing water to 1.2 million people after treatment at one of the largest water works in Europe. Consumption is about 320 million litres every day. Imagine the bill if that was San Pellegrino.

The Cube | The Rotunda | Radisson Blu Hotel | Queen Elizabeth II Hospital

Bartley Reservoir
Water from Wales

Photo taken from a lay-by on Egghill Lane
///driver.sand.heat

Chapter 35

Destroyer of Worlds

You will have read in this book about some of the inventions made in Birmingham or by Brummies. This last main chapter describes what is, perhaps, the biggest thing to ever come out of Birmingham. Though many may wish it never had.

The world changing item wasn't a new machine or device. It was a little-known document. The brief six pages were written in March 1940 and later became referred to as 'The Frisch-Peierls Memorandum'. The full title gives more of a clue to the document's nature; 'Memorandum on the properties of a radioactive "super-bomb"'

The super bomb is what we now call a nuclear or atomic bomb and it was the first time that a theoretical outline for the bomb had been laid down. The lid of the Pandora's Box containing nuclear weapons was prised ajar in a small office at the University of Birmingham where the memorandum was written.

Otto Frisch and Rudolf Peierls were physicists. Frisch was Austrian and Peierls was German, but both had Jewish heritage so had settled in Britain following the rise of Hitler and Nazism. Shortly after the outbreak of World War II they found themselves both working at the University of Birmingham.

Through the Round Window...
... the nightmare of nuclear war began. Inside the small corner office of the Poynting Building furniture and equipment has been retained since Frisch and Peierls worked there. The office is not open to the public.
Campus of the University of Birmingham
///bright.mason.pitch

Whilst nuclear reactors and bombs were not a new concept at the time, it was not thought that a viable weapon could be made. To produce the necessary chain reaction a bomb required large amounts of uranium which is a very dense, heavy metal (if a can of cola were full of uranium it would weigh around the same as six bags of sugar. And be just as bad for your teeth). The amount of uranium required would render a weapon too unwieldy to deploy.

The key to Frisch and Peierls' research at the university was to consider isolating a special, rare form of uranium which they thought could produce a viable weapon in smaller amounts. They were right, and to their amazement the quantity required turned out to be only about the size of a golf ball.

The resulting memorandum gave the technical results of their experiments which are practically impenetrable to a non nuclear physicist. You don't need to be a physicist though to understand the destructive power of the bomb which Frisch and Peierls presented starkly and with considerable foresight given a bomb didn't yet exist.

The memorandum describes how a bomb would produce an explosion the same as 1000 tons of dynamite, incredible heat (the same as the interior of the sun for an instant), destroy life in a wide area, have long lasting and far reaching effects of deadly radiation and that effective protection from the bomb would be 'hardly possible'. They also mooted the idea of the bomb becoming a deterrent.

Following their memorandum, Frisch and Peierls became involved in the race to produce the first nuclear bomb. In the 1940s, when World War II was in full swing, Frisch and Peierls had become British citizens which gave them more freedom to be employed on the most classified projects. They went to work on the top-secret Manhattan Project at the Los Alamos laboratory in the USA. The project's aim was to produce the first atomic weapons and was led by Robert Oppenheimer. On 16th July 1945 the first test ('Trinity Test') of a nuclear bomb was undertaken in New Mexico and Frisch and Peierls were there to see it. It was that first test which prompted Oppenheimer to recall verses from the Hindu scripture Bhagavad Gita: "If the radiance of a thousand suns were to burst at once into the sky, that would be like the splendour of the mighty one..." and "Now I am become Death, the destroyer of worlds".

Within 24 days of the Trinity Test the first nuclear weapons had been used against Japan causing devastation at Hiroshima and Nagasaki.

Nearby Frisch and Peierls' old office, a small, blue plaque is possibly the most understated ever. It simply states 'Otto Frisch and Rudolf Peierls showed the feasibility of an airborne atomic weapon here in 1940'. The magnitude of the destroyer of worlds they had unleashed seems so much more.

Chapter 36

Random Nuggets

Miscellaneous snippets I picked up along the way.

The largest Primark in the world is at the Pavilions in Birmingham City Centre. It is also the largest fashion retail store in the world.

High Street
City Centre
///funny.hints.wash

This is the Miller Pulpit at St Martin in the Bull Ring named after Dr John Miller, a rector here in the 1800s. It is the only one of its kind in the UK.

City Centre
///fled.curl.frost

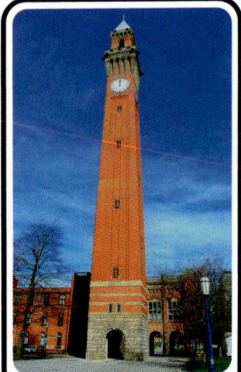

The tallest free-standing clock tower in the world is the Joseph Chamberlain Memorial Clock Tower on the campus of the University of Birmingham. The tower is around 100m high and has the nick name of 'Old Joe'.
Legend has it that students will fail to graduate if they walk through the clock tower whilst it chimes. After a degree is safely in the bag, graduates have been known to deliberately walk through the clock tower whilst the bongs ring out.

University of Birmingham Campus.
///jams.guilty.notes

If you've ever passed by this oversized padlock at the junction of Newhall Hill and Sand Pits wondering what it is, you would find no clues on the padlock itself. The padlock marks the start of the Charm Bracelet Trail – a walking tour of the Jewellery Quarter.

///busy.tulip.heave

There are a couple of oddities about this apartment building in the City Centre:
1. It is called 'The Old Chapel'. It has never been a chapel but housed electrical equipment.
2. Half the building seems to be on St Paul's Square and the other half on Charlotte Street. The official postal address is 57 St Paul's Square. But the letter box is on Charlotte Street.
City Centre
///ripe.valid.narrow

86 | The Quirky Guide to Birmingham

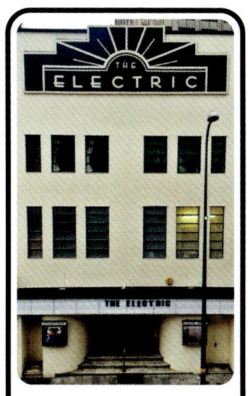

The Electric Cinema in the City Centre is the oldest functioning cinema in the UK.

Station Street
///second.lifts.clubs

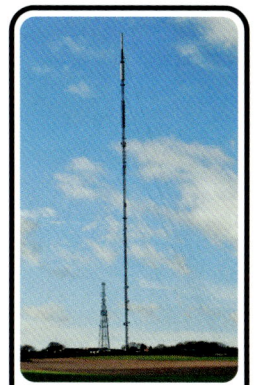

The tallest structure in Birmingham is not the BT tower or The Rotunda. It is the Sutton Coldfield transmitter which stands at some 240m – around 98m taller than the BT Tower.

Lichfield Road, Sutton Coldfield
///mimic.riding.panic

The shortest cycle lane? At less than 15m (49 feet) this lane in Cotteridge must be a contender, providing a few seconds worth of additional protection to cyclists.
There is no other cycle lane on the whole road. The lane markings and new sign post were installed by the council due to a kink in the road.
Cycling groups were not impressed

You'll need to look up to spot this 'Peaky Blinder' lounging on the third floor of the Assay Lofts apartments.

Charlotte Street
City Centre
///freed.behind.hips

Watford Road
Cotteridge
///times.glue.back

Finding out what are the steepest, narrowest and longest public roads in Britain is quite straightforward but finding the public road with lowest headroom in the country is not quite so easy. This must be a contender though. A short tunnel under the railway lines With just a 5'3" (1.6m) clearance. Even Declan Donnelly wouldn't be able to walk through completely upright at the lowest points. Just after the tunnel is a rare opportunity to drive through the River Rea at the only remaining public ford of the river.
The Mill Walk, Northfield.
///verge.gallons.scam

The Quirky Guide to Birmingham | 87

Thin Lizzy front man and son in law of Leslie Crowther, Phil Lynott, is most associated with his Irish heritage. His mother was Irish and he is buried in Dublin where there is also a statue of him on Harry Street. Lynott was actually born in Hallam (now Sandwell) Hospital in West Bromwich (which isn't Birmingham) before moving to the Woodville Mother and Baby Home in Selly Park (Birmingham, phew). He was baptised at St Edward's catholic church, a stroll down the road from the home. He moved to live in Dublin with his grandparents aged around 8. Coincidently, Led Zeppelin vocalist Robert Plant was born on exactly the same date as Lynott a year earlier in the same hospital in West Bromwich. Which still isn't in Birmingham.

Hospice
///scarf.ears.order

St Edward's
///empire.shuts.placed

Local comedian Joe Lycett had his kitchen extension at his Kings Heath home opened by Lord Mayor of Birmingham Yvonne Mosquito in May 2019 and raised thousands for charity in the process.

In 2005 a Red Panda named Babu escaped from Birmingham Wildlife Conservation Park. He was found around a mile away four days later. Babu went on the win 'Brummie of the Year' the same year albeit in a limited poll. Sadly, Babu died in 2013. Current Red Pandas have yet to make a break for freedom.

Pershore Road
///offers.blur.doctor

Digbeth Police Station once hosted some very famous guests. The Beatles played concerts on five occasions in Birmingham in the 1960s. In November 1963 they were due to play at the Birmingham Hippodrome but this visit also involved the Fab Four spending time in the police station. Beatlemania was well established and the police were concerned about how they could safely get the Beatles through the crowds gathered around the theatre. The cunning plan was to smuggle the band into the venue disguised as policemen. The Beatles made the short journey from the police station to the Hippodrome in a police van and alighted wearing traditional police helmets. It was not the first time this ploy had been used in Birmingham. Back in 1901 David Lloyd George was due to give a controversial anti-Boer War speech at the Town Hall. A riot broke out and Lloyd George had to be smuggled out of the venue in a police uniform for fear of his life. Twenty years later, at the same location, he was granted the freedom of the City. Politics eh.

Digbeth, City Centre
///radar.nights.lung

88 | The Quirky Guide to Birmingham

This 'cross with pride' rainbow crossing was created in 2020 to coincide with the city's 'Pride' celebrations which became a casualty of Covid-19. The artist was James Cowper, also known as drag performer Gavina.

Junction of Hurst Street and Ladywell Walk
City Centre
///smug.lost.diary

Firmin & Sons is the self-proclaimed oldest manufacturing company in the UK. It has been going since 1655. They are currently based at New Town Row and have worked with every British monarch since Charles II. Originally a button manufacturer, the company now designs and supplies uniforms, livery and badges for the British military and those of more than thirty other countries.
New Town Row
///escape.sculpture.fork

If you're of a certain age and can still recite the phone number of Swap Shop (01 811 8055) then the postcode B1 2JP may also ring a bell. This was the postcode for 'Tiswas', the madcap children's (allegedly) Saturday morning TV show made in Birmingham in the 1970s and 80s. You could still try to write a letter to Sally James as ITV (Central) still has offices with the same post code on Gas Street in the city centre. No promises it would get to her though.

The first Aldi store in the UK opened in April 1990 in Stechford.

Stechford Lane
///total.vine.venues

The lampposts near the Cadbury factory are painted purple to match the branding of the chocolate company. But then, you'd already know that if you read the introduction to this book. Which nobody does. What better place to end than where it started?

Bournville Lane
Bournville.
///groups.trucks.call

The Quirky Guide to Birmingham | 89

Index

Index

A
Acme 48
Acme Thunderer 48
Acocks Green 56
The Actress and Bishop 22
Adderley St 51
aeronautics 45
Aldi 89
Aldridge Road 57
Allcock St 51
Alpha Tower 18
Ampton Road 60
anchor 58
Anchor Exchange 46
aqueduct 82
Assay Office 58
Aston Villa 31, 64
Athena 61
Athena Studios 61
Atkinson, Peter 61
atomic bomb 84
ATV 79
Austen, Jane 7
Austin, Steve 32

B
Babu 88
Back of Rackhams 14
Bader Walk 45
Banksy 50
Barnes, Rachael 81
Barr St 48
Bartley Green 78
Baskerville House 38
Baskerville, John 38
Baskerville, Sarah 40
Baskerville typeface 39
Battle of Colenso 26
Bayern Munich 65
Beatlemania 88
The Beatles 17, 88
Beaumarchais, Pierre-Augustin Caron de 40
Bedson, Professor Henry 72
beehive 81
Berlin Wall 33
Bhagavad Gita 85
Billboard 17
Billingham, Josh 51
Birmingham Airport 63
Birmingham City FC 31, 64
Birmingham Wildlife Conservation Park 88
Bishop Vesey 68
Blackadder Goes Forth 48
Black Sabbath 16, 17
Bloye, William 15
blue nose 31
Bollard 57
Bond, James 46
Boulton, Matthew 15, 58
boundary markers 74
Bournville Lane 89
Broad Street 17, 65
Bromley St 51
Brummie of the Year 88
BT tower 87
Buckingham Palace 70
Budd, Kenneth 34, 81
Budd, Oliver 34
Bull 10, 11
Bullring 10, 11, 18, 77
Bull Ring 67
Bulpitt & Sons 43
Bunford, Jane 'Ginny' 78
Burma 33
Burnt Norton 21

92 | The Quirky Guide to Birmingham

Busted 32
Butler, Fiona 61
C
Cadbury 89
Camden Street 43
canals 67
Cannon Hill Park 54
Carpenter Road 60
Carpet salesmen 14
Castle Bromwich Aerodrome 44
Castle Bromwich Aircraft Factory 44
Castle Vale 44
Catherine De Barnes 72
Catherines Close 73
Celtic Cross 35
Centenary Square 42
Central Post Office 36
Charlotte Street 86, 87
Charm Bracelet Trail 76, 86
Chester 58
Chester Road 44
Christ Church 41
Churchill, Winston 30
City Centre 4
City of a thousand trades 67
Clangers, The 32, 48
Clay Lane 37
Clock Tower 56, 86
Coat of Arms 70
Columbo 2
Concorde Drive 45
constituency 4
contemporary art 77
Coronation Street 68
Cotteridge 87
Council House 74
Covid-19 51, 72

Cowans, Gordon 65
Cowper, James 89
cross with pride 89
Crown and Anchor 59
Crowther, Leslie 88
Cuban Missile Crisis 46
cycle lane 87
D
Dae, Larry 74
Darwin, Charles 30
Dhamma Talaka Pagoda 33
diamond 54
Diamond Jubilee 31
Diana 20, 30
Digbeth 32, 37, 50, 51
Digbeth Police Station 88
Dixon, Andy 49
Dixon, Nicola 49
Donnelly, Declan 87
Dulverton Road 57
E
Eames, James (Jim) 54
Easy Hill 38
Eaves, Sarah 39
Ebony 74
Eden Place 57
Edgbaston 4, 56, 57, 60
Edgbaston Archery and Lawn Tennis Society 60
Edgbaston Reservoir 33
Edmund Street 74
Edward VIII 36
Elan Valley 82
Electric Cinema 87
Elkington & Co 59, 61
Elliott, Martin 61
Mrs Elton 9, 7, 9
Emma 7

English Football League 64
Erdington 4, 56
European Cup 64, 65
F
FA 48
FA Cup 64, 76
Fairfax School 49
Fattorini & Sons 76
fifty pound note 58
fireworks 77
Firmin & Sons 89
First World War 48
Five Ways 37
Flag 51, 67
Flanagan, Helen 68
Floodgate Street 51
Floozie in the Jacuzzi 20
football 48
ford 87
Formula 1 75
Formula 3 75
The Fox 65
Fox Hollies Road 56
France 76
Frederick Road 57
French Revolution 40
The Frisch Peierls Memorandum 84
Frisch, Otto 84
G
The Gardens 56
Gas Street 89
Gavina 89
GEC Administration Block 57
Gem, Harry 60
Gent 48 51
Gibb Street 51
Gibson, Colin 65
Gibson, Mr 40
Gold, David 64

Golden Boys 15
gold medal 36
Google 71
Grammer, Kelsey 48
Gretna Green 81
Grey, Oswald Augustus 22
The Guardian 51
Guardian, The 11
Guinness Book of Records 62, 78
H
Hack St 51
Hall Green 4
hallmark 58
hanging 22
Hartopp Road 68
Hauptmann, John 79
Heath Mill Lane 51
heating element 43
Helianthus 49
highest numbered house 62
High St Deritend 51
Hill, Rowland 36
Hill St 36
Hippodrome 88
Hiroshima 85
Historic England 56
Hockley Circus 80
Hodge Hill 4
Hollymore Hospital 56
House of Commons 27
House of Fraser 15
Hudson, Joseph 48
Hurst Street 89
Hyatt Hotel 18
I
Icknield St 58
Ikon Gallery 77
Industrial Revolution 58
International Organization for Standardization 43

94 | The Quirky Guide to Birmingham

Iron Mountain 30
ITV 89

J

Jacuzzi 21
Jaguar 44, 45
japanning 38
Jelly Bean 10
Jelly Belly 10
jewellery 54
Jewellery Quarter 50, 58, 61, 80
JFK 34
J Hudson and Co. 48

K

Kennedy, Edward 34
Kennedy, John Fitzgerald 34
Keogh, Thomas 67
Kerrang! 32
kettle 43
Kettleworks 43
King Charles II 68
King George V 28
King Henry VIII 68
King, Martin Luther 34
Kings Heath 88
Kingstanding. 56
kitchen extension 88
Knight, Alfred Joseph 36

L

Ladybird Books 68
Ladywell Walk 89
Ladywood 4, 33
lampposts 89
Lawn Tennis 60
Led Zeppelin 88
Lennon, John 30
Les Misérables 76
The Library of Birmingham 6, 18, 38, 40, 60
Licko, Zuzana 40
listed buildings 57

The Little Tin Idol 64
Little Aston 68
Livery Street 14, 15
Lloyd, Anne (Nancy) 81
Lloyd, Sampson 81
Lloyds Bank 80, 81
Lord Mayor 54, 88
Los Alamos 85
Lower Trinity St 51
lowest headroom 87
Ludgate Hill 22
Lycett, Joe 88
Lynott, Phil 88

M

Manhattan Project 85
manhole covers 75
Markets Car Park 18
Marston, Job 40
Mason, Sir Josiah 31
Master of the House 76
Maxfield, Paul 23
McKenna, John 49
McLennan, Tony 73
Mellotron 17
Meriden Street 51
meteorite 77
metre 76
Milestone 56
The Mill Walk 87
Miller, Dr John 86
Miller Pulpit 86
Mills, Julia 70
Mistry, Dhruva 20
Mitchell, Andrew 68
Mitchell, William 80
Monaco 75
Moon, Keith 32
Moore, Brian 65
Moore, Roger 46
Moor Pool Estate 57

morgue 74
mortuary 74
Moseley 37
Mosquito, Yvonne 88
Mothers Club 17
The Move 17
Mrs Eaves 40
mural 51
Murdoch, William 15
Myanmar 33

N
Nagasaki 85
Nangle, Mike 34
National Football Museum 64
National Isolation Hospital 72
Navigation Street 57
Newhall Hill 76, 86
Newhall Street 59
New Street Station 57
New Town Row 64, 89
No. 11 5
Northfield 4
Northfield giantess 78
Nowakowski, Ondre 31
nuclear bomb 46, 85
nuclear weapons 84

O
Ohel 56
The Old Chapel 86
Old Joe 86
Old Square 81
Olympics 36
Oppenheimer, Robert 85
Orion House 18
Osbourne, Ozzy 17
Outer Circle 5

P
padlock 86
Pandora's Box 84
Paradise Circus 68

Paralympics 36
Parker, Cornelia 77
Parker, Janet 72
passports 36
Peaky Blinder 87
Peel, John 17
Peierls, Rudolf 84
pelota 60
Perera, Augurio 60
Perry Barr 4, 57
Pershore Road 88
Peter and Jane 68
Piccadilly Arcade 23
Pigeon Park 14
pillar box 36
Plant, Robert 88
Play Sculpture 56
Poole, A. John 80
postage stamp 36
postcode 62, 89
Potter, Beatrix 30
Poynting Building 84
President of the United States 35
Priestly Riots 40
Primark 86
Princess of Wales 20, 30
Probate Service 30
pyrotechnics 77

Q
quarantine 72
Queen 70
Queen Elizabeth II 28
Queen Victoria 74

R
Rackhams 15
Racquets 60
rainbow crossing 89
The Ramp 14
Rangoon 33
Ravenhill, George Albert 26

Ravenhurst Rd 57
Ready Player One 15
Red Panda 88
Richard Eaves 39
The River 14, 20
River Rea 87
Roadrunner 48
The Rolling Stones 32
Rotunda 19, 77, 87
Rotunda Relief 80
The Royal Sutton Coldfield Town Council 71
The Royal Town of Sutton Coldfield 69
Royal Charter 68
Royal Highland Fusiliers 29
Royal Observatory 76
Royal Town 68
Rudolph 50

S

Salford Circus 25
Sand Pits 86
Savalas, Telly 18
Second Boer War 26
Secunda, Tony 17
Selfridges 10, 19
Selly Oak 4
Sentinel 44
Severn Trent Water 83
Sheffield 65
Shillcock Grove 64
Shillcock, William 64
Shwedagon Pagoda 33
Sideshow Bob 48
Signal Box 57
Simpsons, The 48
Sinclair, Scott 68
Singapore 75
Sleeping Iron Giant 31
Smallpox 72

Smith, David 67
Solihull 63
Spaghetti Junction 24
Spencer Diamond 54
Spielberg, Steven 15
Spitfire 44
Spitfire Island 44
St Chad's 34
St Chad's Circus 34
Stechford Lane 89
St Edwards 88
St Martin in the Bull Ring 19, 86
St Michaels and All Angels 78
Stocker, Nannette 79
St Paul's Square 86
St Philip's Cathedral 15, 40, 79
Stratford Road 62
studs 74
Summerfield, William 81
sunflower 49
super-bomb 84
Superprix 75
Sutton Coldfield 4, 49, 68
Sutton Coldfield transmitter 87
Sutton Park 68
Swan 43
Swap Shop 89

T

Taylor, John 38, 81
tea 43
Telephone Boxes 57
televisions 32
Temple of Relief 80
Tennant Street 37
Tennis Girl 61
Tessall Lane 56
Thénardier, Monsieur 76
Thinktank 45
Thin Lizzy 88
Timmins, Mr 41

Tiswas 89
Titanic 48, 59
Tolkien, J.R.R. 44
Tolkien, Tim 44
Town Hall 88
Trafalgar Square 76
Trinity Test 85
trompe l'oeil' 23
T.S.Eliot 21
Tudor Rose 69
Tulip Festival 54
Two Towers 15
Typhoo Tea 43

U

underground 46
UNESCO 33
University of Birmingham 61, 78, 84
University of Birmingham Medical School 72
uranium 84
urinal 80

V

Vaughton, Howard 64
Vaughtons 64
Victoria Cross 26, 36, 37
Victoria Square 20, 36, 62, 65, 74, 76
Villa Park 65
Voltaire 40
Vyse Street 50

W

Wales 83
Walk of Stars 65
War Office 27
Warren Road 56
Warstone Lane 58
Warstone Lane Cemetery 41
water supply 83
Water Tower 56

Watt, James 15
Webster, Rosie 68
Westbourne Road 60
West Bromwich 88
West Bromwich Albion 64
whistle 48
White House 35
Wile E Coyote 48
Will 30
Willis, Emma 32
Willis, Matt 32
Wilson, Harold 17
Wimbledon 61
Wimbledon Lawn Tennis Museum 61
Wingfield, Harry 68
Winson Green 22
Witcomb, Frederick 73
Withe, Peter 65
Witton 57
Witton Cemetery 26
Wood, Roy 17
Woodville Mother and Baby Home 88
World Health Organisation 73
World War II 44, 74, 84
Worth, Fred L 2

Y

Yangon 33
Yardley 4, 37
yarn-bombed 31

Z

Zara 80
Zephaniah, Benjamin 11
'Zig Zag' Bridge 57

Tarar a bit, Bab.